Evaluating Models of
Christian Counseling

Evaluating Models of Christian Counseling

GEORGE R. ROSS

WIPF & STOCK · Eugene, Oregon

EVALUATING MODELS OF CHRISTIAN COUNSELING

Copyright © 2011 George R. Ross. All rights reserved. Except for brief quotations in critical publications or reviews, no part of this book may be reproduced in any manner without prior written permission from the publisher. Write: Permissions, Wipf and Stock Publishers, 199 W. 8th Ave., Suite 3, Eugene, OR 97401.

Wipf & Stock
An Imprint of Wipf and Stock Publishers
199 W. 8th Ave., Suite 3
Eugene, OR 97401

www.wipfandstock.com

ISBN 13: 978-1-60899-848-7

Manufactured in the U.S.A.

Contents

Preface / vii

1. The Counseling Process / 1

2. Psychology and the Counseling Process / 11

3. Theology and the Counseling Process / 16

4. Spirituality and the Counseling Process / 22

5. Integrating Psychology, Theology, and Spirituality / 29

6. Evaluating Models of Christian Counseling / 70

7. Jay Adams's Nouthetic Counseling / 79

8. Bill Gothard's Basic Life Principles / 97

9. Robert McGee's Search for Significance / 110

10. Kenneth Haugk's Christian Caregiving / 120

Epilogue / 129
Appendix / 131
Bibliography / 135

Preface

INTENDED TO be used within a course setting, this book challenges the interested student to examine the perplexities present in evaluating how effectively a model of Christian counseling incorporates psychological, theological, and spiritual principles. This book presents an opportunity for the motivated student to develop skills necessary to effectively evaluate models of Christian counseling. A student studying this book will develop sensitivity to the underlying psychological, theological, and spiritual dimensions of four models of Christian counseling, learn how to compare and contrast the strengths and limitations of each model, and learn how to evaluate the efficacy and efficiency of each approach as a legitimate means of counseling.

In the first four chapters of the book a foundation is established. Working definitions of the counseling process, psychology, theology, and spirituality are outlined. Equipped with this set of working definitions, the student is introduced in chapter 5 to several viewpoints outlining the merits, feasibility, and objections to developing a model of Christian counseling that integrates psychology, theology, and spirituality.

In chapter 6 the student is introduced to a carefully crafted three pronged evaluation model designed to unravel the prevailing psychology, theology, and spirituality of any given model of Christian counseling. Chapters 7–10 provide for the student four illustrations on how to apply the evaluation model. Chapter 7 examines the "nouthetic" counseling model of Jay Adams. Chapter 8 evaluates Bill Gothard's "basic life principles" model of Christian counseling. Chapter 9 reviews Robert McGee's "search for significance" model of Christian counseling. Chapter 10 assesses Kenneth Haugk's model of "Christian caregiving."

1

The Counseling Process

IN ORDER to examine the relationships between psychology, theology, and spirituality and their respective interactions within the counseling process, one must first clearly delineate a working definition of these terms. What is the counseling process? What is psychology? What is theology? What is spirituality? McMinn (1996, 9–10) explains: "For Christian counselors doing interdisciplinary integration, two areas of competence are necessary and sufficient: psychology and theology." But if "we are to bring religious issues out of the scholarly journals into the Christian counseling office," we must also "understand spirituality and the process of spiritual formation."

DEFINING THE COUNSELING PROCESS

Oden (1966, 17) understands counseling as a "process of conversation with a congruent human brother who mediates empathetic understanding and unconditional positive regard with a view toward resolving destructive inner conflict." Shertzer and Stone (1968, 22–26) define counseling as "an interaction process which facilitates meaningful understanding of self and environment and results in the establishment and or clarification of goals and values for future behavior." Truax and Carkhuff (1967, 25) contend that the counseling process is earmarked by "three sets of characteristics," "accurate empathy, non-possessive warmth, and genuineness." Every major theory of psychotherapy and counseling stress the "importance of the therapist's ability to be integrated, mature, genuine, authentic or congruent in his relationship to the patient," being able to "provide a non-threatening, trusting, safe or secure atmosphere by his acceptance, non possessive warmth, unconditional positive regard, or love," and demonstrate the ability to be "accurately empathic, be 'with' the client, be understanding, or grasp the patient's meaning."

Eisenberg and Delaney (1977, 72) in their classic work, *The Counseling Process*, contend that "counseling may be seen as a process of a series of stages which include the initial meeting, exploration of client concern and relationship development, goal achievement, development and implementation of an approach to goal achievement, evaluation of results, and termination and follow up." The counseling process is an effort by the counselor to help people "make important decisions . . . deal and cope with crisis situations . . . reduce counterproductive behaviors . . . stimulate healthy individual growth . . . and help in making vocational choices" (14). In short, the counseling process is a growth and enhancement procedure designed to produce "fully functioning" individuals that demonstrate qualities of consistency, commitment, self-control, competence, creativity, and self-awareness.

Individuals are fully functioning when they are *consistent*, that is, when they "behave and make decisions that are reasonably consistent both within social roles, through time, and across social roles" demonstrating "a well-integrated sense of personal identity." Individuals are fully functioning when they demonstrate the quality of *commitment*, that is, when they are "able to commit self to goals and purposes that are enhancing and helpful to self, others, and various groups and organizations ... and to self-transcending values that give meaning and purpose to life and thus protect from hopelessness, obsessive fear of death, and existential despair."

Individuals are fully functioning when *self-control* is demonstrated, that is, when emotions that are expressed are "reasonable in proportion to the situation related to them." Individuals are fully functioning when *competence* is evidenced, as demonstrated when individuals can act "proactively rather than reactively on the environment ... oriented more towards anticipatory problem solving than a crisis coping base." Individuals are fully functioning when they can act with *creativity*. This is evident when individuals are able to "produce something new ... think divergently ... develop unusual and effective solutions to difficult problems." Individuals are fully functioning when *self-awareness* exist, that is, when individuals are "aware of talents, abilities, and limitations ... of the motivations, beliefs, and values, feelings, and assumptions that affect personal behavior and decisions" (15–16).

Bandler and Grinder (1975, 35–38) stress that critical to defining the counseling process is grasping an understanding of the client's language structure. They explain: "When humans wish to communicate their representation, their experience of the world, they form a linguistic representation of the experience ... they make a series of choices transformations about the form in which they will communicate the experience." Therefore, for Bandler and Grinder, the counseling process is about "transformational grammar ... the mechanisms ... in which we represent our experience." The semantic meaning, they explain, "which these processes represent, is existential, infinitely rich and varied," and "the meta model is an explicit representation of our unconscious, rule-governed behavior." The counseling process is about what linguists have described as the "representational system called language." It is about *deletion*, when we "selectively pay attention to certain dimensions of our experience and exclude others." It is about *distortion*, when we "make shifts in our experience of sensory data," for example, using fantasy. It is about *generalization*, when "elements or pieces of a person's model become detached from their original experience and come to represent the entire category of which the experience is an example" (14–16).

Bandler and Grinder (1976, 195) conclude that "all forms of therapy, all the techniques of the different forms of therapy—in fact, all learning—can be understood in terms of the process of representation. All the techniques of every form of therapy are techniques which affect the processes of representation, the creation and organization of a client's model of the world." Change becomes contingent upon changing the client's model of the world. As a client's model of the world changes, perceptions change, and so too does behavior. An impoverished representation can be reshaped into one of enrichment. Therefore, the counseling process encompasses our representational systems, our differing ways "of representing our experiences of the world" (6). Consequently, having understood how a client "organizes his experience, which representational system is used and which is the client's most highly valued one," strategies can be employed to expand a "client's model of the world in a way which will allow him more choices, greater freedom in living, and a richer life overall" (25).

Brammer (1973, 55–79) in his classic work, *The Helping Relationship: Process and Skills*, identifies the counseling process as a helping affiliation for the express purpose of assisting someone to understand a problem, being supportive in the midst of the problem, and/or aiding the person in developing a positive action in response to the identified problem or problems. He explains that "from a generalist helper point of view, there are eight stages in the helping process." They include: *entry* ("opening the relationship"), *clarification* ("stating the problem or concern and reason for seeking help"), *structure* ("formulating the contract"), *relationship* ("building the helping relationship"), *exploration* ("exploring problems, formulating goals, planning strategies, gathering facts, expressing deeper feelings, learning new skills"), *consolidation* ("exploring alternatives, working through feelings, practicing new skills"), *planning* ("developing a plan of action, using strategies to resolve conflicts, reducing painful feelings, and consolidating and generalizing new skills or behaviors to continue self-directed activities"), and termination ("evaluating outcomes and terminating the relationship"). Therefore, the counseling process incorporates models of "problem solving, skill development, and life planning."

The counseling process also requires the development and employment of special skills. Essential skills needed for promoting "understanding" in the counseling process include skills of listening, leading, reflecting, summarizing, confronting, interpreting, and informing. Essential skills needed for promoting "comfort and crisis utilization" in the counseling process include the skills of supporting, crisis intervening, centering, and referring. Essential skills needed for promoting "positive action" in the counseling process include skills of problem solving, decision making, and behavior modification.

Dyer and Vriend (1975, 17–20) regard the counseling process as "an interpersonal helping procedure which begins with client exploration for purposes of identifying thinking, feeling and doing processes which are in any way self-defeating or require upgrading." The process involves the counselor helping the client "determine and declare counterproductive behaviors . . . set goals . . . identify significant self-logic and self-performance wherein thinking, feeling, and doing are evidently self-defeating." The counseling process involves moving "the client toward self-understanding . . . to explore possible alternatives to the self-defeating thinking, feeling, and doing," helping the client "incorporate new thinking" with "total emphasis on the acquisition and incorporation into the self-system of productive new behaviors." At the core of their understanding of the counseling process is the assumption that "each client's data are unique, personally owned, and of a particular character having personal meaning and value." They also assume that in the context of the counseling process the "counselor is the skilled and competent person in the relationship and the interpersonal helping activity, and to the extent the counselor is less skilled or competent than the client in a given behavior dimension, counseling will be unproductive, even abusive to the client."

Adams (1979, ix) defines the counseling process in terms of change. He explains: "As diverse as the various counseling systems may be—and they are quite distinct fundamentally—they all (1) see a need for change and (2) use verbal means to bring about change, which (3) is purported to be for the benefit of the counselee."

Ivey and Downing (1980, 4–13) explain that counseling is "a process of interpersonal influence . . . concerned with assisting normal people to achieve their goals or function more effectively." It is a process of helping people achieve goals of "self-actualization, development of an increased ability to respond and cope, the ability to love and work, to do one's own thing, or to be truly oneself."

Collins (1988, 38–48) explains that counseling is "not a step-by-step process like baking a cake or changing a tire"; nonetheless, he contends, several steps are involved in helping people deal with "problems, attitudes, values, expectations, and experiences." He has identified five phases in the counseling process that include: *connecting* ("initiating, building and maintaining a relationship"), *exploring* ("enabling the client to 'tell their stories'"), *planning* ("goals and actions that can be taken to find solutions"), *progressing* ("start moving toward their goals"), and *stopping* ("summarizing what has been learned and accomplished" as the counseling comes to an end). Conducted in an environment that emphasizes "warmth, genuineness, and empathy," Collins suggests that counseling is a process used to help clients gain self-understanding, learn effective patterns of communication, discover more effective ways of responding, learn to achieve one's "optimal potential," and perhaps most importantly, realize "spiritual wholeness."

Jones and Butman (1991, 12) describe the counseling process "as a dyadic two-way interaction between a client who is distressed, and perhaps confused and frightened, and a professional helper whose helping skills are recognized and accepted by the client." They explain that the process is a "private, collaborative encounter" that relies "heavily on verbal communication of the client's thoughts, feelings, attitudes, and behaviors." Hope is fostered by the therapist's ability to understand, explain and apply techniques that reduce the client's distress. These techniques include "offering reassurance and support, desensitizing the client to distress, encouraging adaptive functioning, and offering understanding and insight."

Bufford (1997, 111–12) argues that the counseling process needs to "address biological factors, including diseases, and endocrinological, anatomical, biochemical, and genetic causes." In addition it should address "psychological factors, including personal, developmental, and family history, and relationships with others." Furthermore, "social factors such as societal and cultural norms and standards" need to be considered. And finally, "spiritual factors, including personal sin, ethical and moral responsibilities, relationship to God, and spiritual growth and development" are essential factors in need of consideration. However, Bufford is careful to distinguish between mental health counseling and spiritual counseling, explaining that mental health counseling "seeks to alleviate conditions which make intervention medically necessary"—typically as reflected by DSM diagnoses—whereas spiritual counseling is "centrally concerned with evangelism and discipleship."

Bridger and Atkinson (1998, 21–22) understand the counseling process "as a one-to-one exercise in which the purpose of the counselor is to relieve mental and emotional distress by restoring internal psychological equilibrium." They further contend that in addition to the counselee's inner world the counseling process "must take account of the differing but related context in which human beings find themselves" Both the social contexts and the psychological contexts are interwoven. In addition, they argue that "neither psychological nor social contexts can be divorced from philosophy and theology." The counseling process must equip the counselee "to face critical questions with theological as well as psychological resources." They conclude their discussion by emphasizing that the counseling process consists of four levels. They range from a "kind of help given by caring persons" to a "deeper analysis and understanding" where "some degree of technical training is required," to where considerable training and expertise is required as "understanding the realm of the unconscious" is undertaken, or in-depth therapy is utilized to achieve "thorough ongoing behavioral change."

WORKING DEFINITION

In summary, the counseling process can be conceptualized as a growth and enhancement experience whereby a highly skilled professional assists individuals in implementing changes in thoughts, feelings, and behaviors, for the purpose of improving one's well-being, alleviating stress or maladjustment, resolving crisis, and increasing one's abilities to live a more highly functional life. Key to the process is the ability of the trained helper to exhibit empathy, warmth, and genuineness toward the individual seeking help as well as the skill to introduce paradigms that will help the counselee identify, understand, and change dysfunctional patterns of thought, that is, linguistic representations of life that significantly interfere with the healthy physical, emotional, and spiritual functioning of the individual.

FUEL FOR THOUGHT

1. What skills does a counselor need to effectively participate in the counseling process?

2. How does a counselor determine whether the client is benefiting from the counseling being received?

3. How does Christian counseling differ from secular counseling?

4. What would you add to or delete from the proposed working definition of the counseling process?

5. What linguistic representations of life do you currently find significantly interfere with your physical, emotional, and spiritual functioning?

2

Psychology and the Counseling Process

DEFINITION OF PSYCHOLOGY

VANDE KEMPE'S (1996, 72) revelation that "psychology and religion have historically been inextricably intertwined" may surprise many twentieth and twenty-first-century psychologists who were taught "a complex of origin myths concocted to bolster the view that psychology was a science unfettered by the bonds of philosophy and theology." But in reality, the Latin origin of the word *psychologia*, first used by Maruic in 1524, "referred to one of the subdivisions of pneumatology that emphasized 'the human spirit'" and later referred to the "doctrine of the human mind." Furthermore, Bridger and Atkinson (1998, 56) cite evidence that the origin of psychology can be traced to the "metaphysical speculations of Greek science in which there was no rigid distinction between philosophical questions of meaning and purpose and scientific study of matters of fact." In fact, despite the rise of modern science in the seventeenth and eighteenth centuries that shifted emphasis in psychology to the "mechanical operation of the mind" and its scientific study, nineteenth-century students of psychology still found it difficult to make "a clear distinction between the pneuma, the spirit or religious aspect of the person, and the psyche, the soul or the psychological." They still continued to struggle with the study of the mind through introspection.

The first two decades of the twentieth century, however, witnessed a major paradigm shift in psychology. The focus of psychology moved away from the study of the mind through introspection and asking questions about meaning and purpose to a science that focused solely on behavior. Spearheaded by the strong influence of John B. Watson at Hopkins University, by 1913 psychology was being transformed into a subject entirely defined in behavioral terms. Watson was claiming that the goal of psychology was the "prediction and control of behavior." By the early 1930s, the subject of introspection and reference to "mind" and "consciousness" had ceased in most psychological textbooks and theoretical discussions. What was to be known as experimental psychology had emerged to the forefront.

Although remnants of the notions of "mind" and "consciousness" could be uncovered in some sources, for the most part, by the early 1960s, behaviorism, in the form of Skinnerian psychology, prevailed. Most textbooks were defining psychology solely in behavioral terms. Even as late as 1979, Morgan, King, and Robinson's text, *Introduction to Psychology,* defined psychology as "the science of human and animal behavior" (Morgan et al. 1979, 4).

The last two decades of the twentieth century have witnessed yet another paradigm shift. Attempts to reintroduce the notions of "mind and consciousness" have regained a foothold in academic circles. Today psychology is most often defined as "the study of behavior and underlying mental phenomena" (Gleitman 1995, 1). In the fourth edition of his text on psychology, Gleitman writes, "What is psychology? It is a field of inquiry that is sometimes defined as the science of the mind, sometimes as the science of behavior. It concerns itself with how and why organisms do what they do." "The scope of psychology," he elaborates, "covers an enormous range." Psychological phenomena "border on biology . . . touch on social sciences such as anthropology and sociology . . . concern behavior in animals . . . pertain to behavior in humans . . . are about conscious experience . . . what people do regardless of what they may feel or think inside."

In reality, however, "psychology is more and more meaningfully defined in terms of the particular field under study rather than as a whole, making it less of a unified discipline and more an umbrella for a loose confederation of sub-disciplines" (APA 1999). This is particularly evident in the fact that the American Psychological Association now serves as host to fifty-five divisions ranging from experimental, clinical, counseling, and school psychology to theoretical and philosophical psychology and psychology and religion.

WORKING DEFINITION

For purposes of this discussion, the more recent conceptualizations of psychology, that of being defined as "the study of behavior and underlying mental phenomena," will be adopted. In addition, the focus of this discussion will be limited to the psychological sub-branches of clinical and counseling psychology. Inquiry will center on the application of the findings of clinical and counseling psychology as applied to the assessment, diagnosis, prediction, prevention, and treatment of psychopathology, mental disorders, and other individual or group problems. Examination will spotlight the use and application of psychological procedures developed specifically to improve behavior adjustment, adaptation, personal effectiveness, and satisfaction. Psychological principles that foster sound mental, emotional, and behavioral health will also be addressed. These include psychological principles that help people improve their well-being, alleviate stress or maladjustment, resolve crisis, and increase their abilities to live a more highly functional life (APA 2001).

CONTEMPORARY PSYCHOTHERAPIES

Jones and Butman (1991) categorize modern psychotherapies into four classifications: dynamic psychologies, behavioral psychologies, humanistic psychologies, and family systems psychologies. Dynamic psychologies include classical psychoanalysis, contemporary psychodynamic psychotherapies, and Jungian therapy. Behavioral psychologies include behavioral, rational-emotive, cognitive-behavioral, Adlerian, and reality therapy. Humanistic psychologies include transactional analysis, person-centered, existential, and gestalt therapy. Family systems psychologies include various forms of family therapy.

It is important to note that as essential tools for clinical and counseling psychologists, the modern psychotherapies "are deeply imbedded in certain world views and control beliefs, especially about the nature of persons and the way good science proceeds" (31). For example, cognitive-behavioral therapies are rooted in Greek Stoic philosophy, classical empiricism, American pragmatism, and functionalism. In contrast, humanistic therapies are embedded in existentialism and romanticism. Family systems and dynamic therapies are heavily influenced by classical empiricism and European Freudian psychology.

FUEL FOR THOUGHT

1. Would psychology be better defined as prediction and control of behavior?
2. How do theories of counseling differ from religious doctrine?
3. What is the difference between a psychological and a spiritual problem?
4. What can psychology tell us about the nature of humanity?
5. Is psychology a science?

3

Theology and the Counseling Process

DEFINITION OF THEOLOGY

THE *WESTMINSTER Dictionary of Theological Terms* (1996, 279–80) defines theology as "language or discourse about God." Elaborating, it explains that theology "can be a scientific, methodological attempt to understand God's divine revelation." Classically, it has been defined as "faith seeking understanding." Macon (1997, 1) contends that "everyone has a theology. Theology simply describes that body of doctrines/concepts which one has surrounding the subject of Deity." Macon further explains that "atheists have a God-less theology. Agnostics have a God-uncertain theology. Theological liberals have a man-centered theology." Bridger and Atkinson (1998, 123) view theology as "a systematic way of expressing our knowledge of God and God's way," stressing that, "as with all human knowing—there is a constant conversation between experience and theory, between belief and practice." The *Columbia Electronic Encyclopedia* (2007) defines the use of the term theology in Christianity as "the systematic study of the nature of God and God's relationship with humanity and with the world."

Thomas Oden (1987, 3–6) in his definitive work, *The Living God*, explains that theology, from the Latin word *theologia*, "comes from two crucial Greek root words: *theos*, God, and *logos*, discourse, language study." Therefore, Oden explains, theology is "reasoned discourse about God gained either by rational reflection or by response to God's self-disclosure in history." Christian theology, Oden clarifies, "is the orderly exposition of Christian teaching. It sets forth that understanding of God that is made known in Jesus Christ." It seeks to provide a coherent reflection on the living God as understood in the community whose life is "in Christ." Emphasizing that Christian theology "presupposes the study of Scripture and of the history of the community's reflection upon Scripture," Oden spells out that the essential purpose of Christian theology "is to study and bring into a fitting, consistent expression the Christian faith" as it seeks "to provide a fit ordering of scriptural teachings and of central themes of the history of scriptural interpretation." Oden further emphasizes that the object in theology is "God as known in the faith of a living community." Theology's task, then, he explicates, "is neither logical demonstration nor normative proclamation of established truth, nor the refining of rigorous proofs of faith," but the task is "clarification of faith's understanding of itself and its ground." This clarification, Oden explains, "asks for fair-minded analysis, critical reasoning, tolerance, and logical coherence, as well as active listening to Scripture and tradition."

Oden (1987, 366–70) explains that four primary divisions of theological study earmark our discourse about God. Theological divisions of reflection include biblical, historical, systematic, and pastoral theology. Biblical or exegetical theology "confines itself primarily to the Scriptures for its textual materials . . . biblical theology . . . seeks to relate and combine the teaching of various Scriptures and bring them into a cohesive doctrinal formulation." Historical theology "studies the development of reflection upon biblical teachings from the time of the apostles to the present." Historical theology embraces "not only the thought of the Christian community but also its institutions, ethos, social life, ethics, law, and liturgies in their development." It also traces "the development of Christian teaching through controversies and through challenging historical conditions." Historical theology remains "essentially a multigenerational commentary and debate on texts of Scripture." Systematic theology "uses the resources of exegetical and historical theology in seeking to build a consistent view of God, utilizing both general human knowledge and the witness to revelation." Systematic theology may embrace constructive theology, apologetics, polemical theology, comparative theology, symbolic theology, ecumenical theology, and irenic theology. It also encompasses moral theology, theological ethics, and Christian social ethics. Systematic theology involves the development of a doctrine of God (theology proper), a doctrine of the universe (cosmology), a doctrine of Christ (Christology), a doctrine of the Holy Spirit (pneumatology), a doctrine of the church (ecclesiology), a doctrine of humanity (anthropology), a doctrine of sin (harmartiology), a doctrine of salvation (soteriology), and a doctrine of last things (eschatology). Pastoral theology "builds upon the exegetical, historical, and systematic theology to provide an understanding of the practice of ministry and of the practical application of the fruits of theology to the work of ministry." It includes homiletics, catechetical theology, liturgics, pastoral care, and church administration.

WORKING DEFINITION

For the purposes of this discussion, theology will be defined as "reasoned discourse about God gained either by rational reflection or by response to God's self-disclosure in history." It "is the orderly exposition of Christian teaching." It sets forth an understanding of God that is "made known in Jesus Christ." In addition, the focus of this discussion will be limited to the theological sub-branches of systematic and pastoral theology. Inquiry will center on the application of the findings of these theologies as applied to the assessment, diagnosis, prediction, prevention, and treatment of psychopathology, mental disorders, and other individual or group problems. Examination will spotlight the application of theological procedures developed to improve behavior adjustment, adaptation, personal effectiveness, and satisfaction. Theological principles that foster sound mental, emotional, and behavioral health will also be discussed. These include principles that help people improve their well-being, alleviate stress or maladjustment, resolve crisis, and increase their abilities to live a more highly functional life.

CONTEMPORARY THEOLOGIES

Smith (1992) divides modern theologies into three major classifications. One group he labels basic contemporary theologies. These "foundational theologies" include fundamentalism, neo-orthodoxy, Pentecostalism, evangelicalism, neo-liberalism, post-Vatican II Catholicism, Eastern Orthodox theology, and the charismatic movement. His second major category he identifies as contemporary world trends. These more "esoteric theologies" include: the theology of hope, process theology, secular theology, theologies of success, liberation theology, third-wave theology, feminist theology, reconstructionist theology, the new age movement, and creation spirituality. His third major classification he tags third world theologies. These theologies include John S. Mbiti's and E. Bolaji Idowu's African theologies and the "water buffalo" and yin-yang theologies of Asia.

It is important to note that each of these three categories of theology can be traced to specific historical campgrounds of theological thought. Each theology examined also contains different underlying doctrinal tenets especially with regards to a doctrine of God, cosmology, Christology, pneumatology, ecclesiology, anthropology, harmartiology, soteriology, and eschatology. For example, fundamentalism was an early twentieth-century Christian movement to "preserve and promote conservative, biblical, Christian orthodoxy" (11). It emphasized the inerrancy and infallibility of Scripture, the virgin birth and deity of Jesus, substitutionary atonement, the literal, physical resurrection of Jesus, and the literal, physical return of Christ.

In contrast, neo-liberalism was a twentieth-century outgrowth that challenged the traditional liberalism fathered by Friedrich Schleiermacher and the Enlightenment intellectuals. It hoped "to apply the gospel practically in everyday life, to make it what it was intended to be—not an academic exercise, but a way of life" (84). But at the same time, neo-liberalism continued to cling to Enlightenment thinking with an ever-increasing tendency to embrace natural theology. This resulted in a suspicion of the supernatural claims of Scripture, thereby challenging, and in many instances abandoning, conservative Christian and orthodox proclamations.

FUEL FOR THOUGHT

1. What are some of the theological principles that foster sound mental, emotional, and behavioral health?

2. What does it mean to define theology as "faith seeking understanding?"

3. What is the difference between a theological liberal and a theological conservative?

4. To what extent does your Christology impact your theology?

5. How does the Bible teach us about the character of God?

4

Spirituality and the Counseling Process

DEFINITION OF SPIRITUALITY

THE *WESTMINSTER Dictionary of Theological Terms* (1996, 268) defines spirituality as "the quality of being spiritual, pertaining to the spirit or nonmaterial." "Historically," it explains, "varieties of spiritualities have emerged relating to different religious traditions. They take place through rituals and practices." Miller and Thoresen (1999, 5–9) point out that "for at least as long as history has been recorded, humankind has assumed that reality is not limited to the material, sensory world." And in the people we counsel, they emphasize, spiritual reality, "be it belief in a supreme being or order, life after physical death, an ultimate reality, or supernatural beings like angels or demons," is an important factor and often serves as an important source of strength and direction in their lives.

Further elaborating, Miller and Thoresen explain that spirituality is complex. "It is not," they contend, "adequately defined by any single continuum or by dichotomous classifications," but is better explained "as multidimensional space in which every individual can be located." Differentiating spirituality from religion, Miller and Thoresen clarify that spirituality is an attribute of individuals whereas religions are organized entities that "focus more on prescribed beliefs, rituals, and practices as well as institutional features." In contrast, spiritual factors "are concerned more with individual subjective experiences, sometimes shared with others." Religion, they explain, "is characterized in many ways by its boundaries and spirituality by a difficulty in defining its boundaries." Religion is an organized social institution with specific beliefs about "how one relates to that which is sacred or divine." Spirituality, in contrast, is often "a highly personal and private matter, focusing on intangible elements that provide vitality and meaning" to life. In short, "clearly, spirituality and religion are not the same." Also, they caution, "words are unquestionably inadequate to fully describe so complex a phenomenon, and, being defined in distinction from material reality, spirituality is particularly difficult to define."

Kurtz (1999, 19–21) reports that Wulff's (1996, 47) notion of spirituality as a term to denote "certain positive inward qualities and perceptions" while avoiding the implications of "narrow, dogmatic beliefs and obligatory religious observances," seems to summarize the current thinking about how to define spirituality. Kurtz elaborates: "The goal of spirituality is the alleviation of mental, emotional, and spiritual distress thought to be at least in part caused by a lack of an appropriate relationship with ultimate reality, most often signaled by and reflected in inappropriate relationships with other people or things." Kurtz emphasizes that "any spirituality is a lived theology, a posture that positions one within total reality," for spirituality embraces "sanity, sanctity, serenity, health, wholeness, and holiness." Spirituality therefore is "an attitude, a posture of one's very being that allows seeing not different things but everything differently." Simply stated, spirituality is that "for which all persons strive."

Eisendrath and Miller (2000, 1–7) define spirituality in the broadest sense as "anything that seems to enhance the sense of the sacred in human life." They explain that spiritual answers are required to questions such as, "Who are we as humans? What is our purpose here? What is the meaning of death in our lives? Can we develop an enduring sense of meaning?"

Mature spirituality, they elaborate, is when a person develops the components of integrity, wisdom, and transcendence. Integrity involves "an ethical commitment and an integration of diverse states," developing "a complex, multifaceted perspective on life and humanity." Wisdom entails qualities "associated with spiritual leaders" that may require the study of both ancient Western philosophical teaching and Eastern philosophies of Buddhism, or may simply "take on an appearance that fits with our experiences of contemporary people." Transcendence encompasses "extending or expanding the limits of our ordinary consciousness or experience in ways that connect us with a symbolic or phenomenal reality beyond the ordinary," going "beyond our common world reality." Spiritual development therefore involves "a lifetime of engagement with a transcendent source that is intimate and Other." Mature spirituality is the "honing of integrity, wisdom, and transcendence in the service of the question of what it means to be human in the Otherness of our universe."

Emmons (1999, 178) stresses the importance of life outcomes as he grapples with "a psychology of spiritual possibilities of what makes life meaningful, valuable, and purposeful." "Spirituality," he explains, "is typically defined broadly, with the term encompassing a search for meaning, for unity, connectedness, for transcendence, for the highest human potential" (92).

Spirituality focuses on the "ultimate purpose and meaning in life." It searches for "a set of principles and ethics to live by, commitment to God or a higher power, recognition of transcendence in everyday experience, a selfless focus, and a set of beliefs and practices that is designed to facilitate a relationship with the transcendent."

Emmons emphasizes that a "common core meaning of spirituality" embraces "the recognition of a transcendent meta empirical dimension of reality." Or as Martin and Carlson (1988) point out, "Spirituality is a process by which individuals recognize the importance of orienting their lives to something nonmaterial that is beyond or larger than themselves . . . so that there is an acknowledgement of and at least some dependence upon a higher power" (59). Emmons (94) concludes that spirituality manifests itself in our spiritual strivings, or what he describes as our attempts "to identify what is sacred or worthy to be committed to." Spiritual strivings "can be conceptualized as ultimate concerns . . . that in which maximal value is invested, which possesses the power to center one's life, and which demands total surrender."

WORKING DEFINITION

For the purposes of this discussion, spirituality will be viewed as the "search for the sacred" as especially demonstrated in our spiritual strivings to discover and embrace ultimate concerns in our lives. Inquiry will center on the discovery of ultimate concerns and their application to the assessment, diagnosis, prediction, prevention, and treatment of psychopathology, mental disorders, and other individual or group problems. Examination will spotlight the application of ultimate concerns to improve behavior adjustment, adaptation, personal effectiveness, and satisfaction. Spiritual principles that foster sound mental, emotional, and behavioral health will also be discussed. These include principles that help people improve their well-being, alleviate stress or maladjustment, resolve crisis, and increase their abilities to live a more highly functional life.

SPIRITUAL INTELLIGENCE

Emmons (1999, 163–76) introduces the notion of spiritual intelligence, defining it as "a framework for identifying and organizing the skills and abilities needed for adaptive use of spirituality." Elaborating, Emmons explains that at a minimum, spiritually intelligent individuals demonstrate the capacity for transcendence; show an ability to enter into heightened spiritual states of consciousness; are able to invest in everyday activities, events, and relationships with a sense of the sacred or the divine; utilize spiritual resources to solve problems in living; and display a capacity to be virtuous and compassionate by exhibiting forgiveness and expressing gratitude while remaining humble.

The first two components, Emmons explains, "deal with the capacity for a person to engage in heightened or extraordinary forms of consciousness," whereas sanctification, setting apart for a special, holy, or godly purpose, encapsulates the third component. The fourth characteristic, the ability to utilize spiritual resources to solve life problems, often involves a conversion experience and the ability to reprioritize goals. The fifth characteristic, the capacity to develop virtues or character traits, comes close to defining who we really are. Collectively, these five components of spiritual intelligence enable spirituality to be viewed "as a set of skills, resources, capacities, or abilities" and provide an "interpretative context for addressing important concerns in daily life."

For the purposes of this discussion, emphasis will center on the fourth and fifth characteristics of spiritual intelligence. Spiritual resources will include prayer, meditation, Scripture, solitude, service, confession, sanctification, worship, surrender, acceptance and forgiveness, hope, serenity, the love of God, the grace of our Lord Jesus Christ, and the fellowship of the Holy Spirit. Virtues or character traits will include gratitude, humility, surrender, forgiveness, serenity, faith, hope, and love.

FUEL FOR THOUGHT

1. Toward what purposes shall I direct my time, energy, and resources?

2. What rules of engagement should I incorporate into my life?
3. What virtues should I strive to emulate?
4. How should I reconcile the imperfections of others?
5. What constitutes life and what constitutes death?

5

Integrating Psychology, Theology, and Spirituality

IN THE first four chapters, working definitions of the counseling process, psychology, theology, and spirituality have been introduced. Schools of thought within each division of inquiry have also been identified. In this chapter, the compatibility of psychology, theology, and spirituality is examined within the context of the counseling process. The focus of inquiry shifts to a discussion of the challenges that emerge when attempting to incorporate each into an integrated counseling approach.

In psychological terminology, the theological notion of sin is described as failure, guilt is replaced by self-awareness, atonement becomes resolution, and redemption is changed to self-acceptance. The question that emerges, however, is whether these psychological descriptions are synonymous with the theological terms they replace, or whether these terms convey different meanings within the framework of psychology. Stated differently, is there a marked difference in a psychological description and understanding of human beings and their needs when contrasted with a theological description and understanding of human beings and their needs? Specifically, how does one's approach to counseling differ if one's frame of reference is psychological rather than theological or vice versa? How does bringing a psychological perspective to the counseling process differ from approaching the process from a theological perspective? Or does it even matter, that is, are the two fields of inquiry compatible? Do both fields of inquiry result in parallel conclusions with their respective terminologies conveying equivalent meanings?

Hunsinger (1995, 6–7), in her book, *Theological and Pastoral Counseling: A New Interdisciplinary Approach*, presents a persuasive argument that psychology and theology are not compatible. She contends that they "represent material that cannot be integrated into a unified whole." Elaborating, she writes, "They are logically diverse; they have different aims, subject matters, methods, and linguistic conventions." Conceding the fact that both perspectives are "integrated into the person" and are "existentially connected," Hunsinger explains "that as language and thought worlds, they are not to be integrated with one another in any systematic way . . . one could not systematically correlate the two." She aptly concludes that each perspective "is understood to offer categories of perception and discernment in the counseling situation . . . each has a vocabulary that pertains to diagnosis and treatment . . . they may each illumine aspects of the self and its situation, . . . and analogies might be drawn between them," but, she emphasizes "they are not really talking about the same thing." She explains that "it is one thing, for instance, to think of oneself as beset with a terrible negative mother complex and as needing to learn to trust one's feminine side," but it is "quite another to think of oneself as mistrusting God's providential goodness and needing to confess the sin of unbelief." But she asks might not "both ways of conceiving one's predicament" be apt in a particular case? Therefore, Hunsinger concludes, fluency in the usage of both the language of psychology and theology will result in more "differentiated perceptions . . . more apt questions, and at least theoretically, more helpful interpretations."

Hunsinger (1995, 61–75) attempts to clarify the relationship between theology and psychology and solidify her position by introducing what she refers to as the "Chalcedonian pattern." Developed in the fifth century "to sort through various Christological controversies and to guide the church in its understanding of Jesus Christ as both human and divine," this complex pattern of reasoning has been used by the noted theologian Karl Barth to examine a wide range of doctrinal or substantive questions. Three significant features of the Chalcedonian pattern include "indissoluble differentiation," "inseparable unity," and "indestructible order." Indissoluble differentiation means that terms are "related without confusion or change." Inseparable unity means that the terms "coincide in an occurrence without separation or division." And indestructible order means that "in and with their differentiated unity, the two are asymmetrically related, with the one term having logical precedence over the other."[1] Therefore, the "two terms are thus differentiated, unified, and ordered in a particular way."

1. Hunsinger explains that logical priority or precedence pertains to the question of "priority in definition." "*A* is logically prior to *B* . . . when the definition of *B* mentions *A*, but the definition of *A* does not mention *B*."

To illustrate Barth's usage of the Chalcedonian pattern, Hunsinger cites Barth's analysis of Mark 2:8–12, where the storyline deals with Jesus's forgiveness and healing of the paralytic. Hunsinger concludes that all three aspects of the Chalcedonian pattern (the unity of forgiveness and healing, the clear differentiation between them, and the asymmetrical order of their relation) are all present in his interpretation of the story. She explains that "healing and forgiveness are seen to occur in a differentiated unity. They occur together, yet each remains distinct differentiation, and the divine power to forgive sins is understood as conceptually prior to and independent of the act of healing ordering." Elaborating, she stresses that "the healing points as a sign to the forgiveness in a way that the forgiveness does not in turn point to the healing." Therefore, she explains, "the divine act of forgiveness is seen as being free and unconditioned, while the healing is seen as existing in the service of Jesus's power to forgive sins. The concepts are so ordered that the forgiveness is logically prior and the healing is logically subsequent."

Hunsinger reasons that "the kind of definitional or logical priority that we are speaking of, therefore, clearly has to do with the arrangement of therapeutic concepts in relation to theological beliefs." Further explaining, she writes, "From a Barthian perspective, the significance of healing is logically subsequent to salvation because although salvation does not necessarily point to healing, healing can be defined as ultimately pointing to salvation."

This fact, she concludes, "will have far-reaching implications for developing a Barthian approach to interdisciplinary relationships between theology and psychology," because from a Barthian position, "although psychological categories are both logically independent of *and* dependent on theological categories in different ways, theological categories are by definition both logically prior to and independent of psychological categories with respect to their significance."

Hunsinger (69) qualifies her conclusion by pointing out that what is at question "are logical relationships that pertain to *concepts*." She explains: "We are speaking of theological and psychological concepts, not directly of theological and psychological *realities*. In reality, there is no reason why these factors may not all come together at one time." Emphasizing that any particular event may have both psychological and spiritual or theological aspects at the same time, "the presence of the former aspects would not invalidate the significance of the latter, nor would the presence of the latter aspects invalidate the significance of the former." She explains that "although they could be conceptually differentiated, they could not finally be separated or divided from one another." She concludes, "At one level the psychological aspects would be significant within a larger pattern of meaning. The spiritual or theological aspects, on the other hand, would be significant in themselves as well as for the way in which they would establish the larger pattern of meaning within which the psychological aspects were ordered."

Hunsinger is also quick to point out the asymmetrical nature of the relationship between psychology and theology. She explains that "the relationship between healing as the sign and salvation as the thing signified is not only analogical but also asymmetrical." She further elaborates: "Although healing points to salvation, the relationship is not reversible, as though salvation would also point in the same sense to healing." "The relationship would be symmetrical and therefore reversible," she emphasizes, "only if the two were essentially or materially equivalent." But, she explains, "healing and salvation are not so equivalent, for they occur on two different levels and indicate two different contexts of meaning. Whereas the significance of the one is temporal, the significance of the other is eternal; whereas the one is penultimate, the other is ultimate." She further argues that "the relationship of signifier to the signified cannot be reversed without effacing this important difference in levels." She explains that "the theological significance of salvation can be stated without reference to healing, but the theological significance of healing cannot be stated without reference to salvation." She therefore concludes that "the significance of salvation as the ultimate term is thus independent of that of healing as the penultimate term, but the relationship is irreversible, for the significance of the penultimate depends on that of the ultimate." The significance of salvation is logically prior to that of healing. "Salvation thus sets the terms within which to think of healing but not as the asymmetry requires us to add the reverse."

Hunsinger reasons that any proposal that attempts to examine the compatibility of psychology with theology must address the "formal features of the Chalcedonian pattern—unity, integrity, and asymmetry." Any such proposal must address "the 'indissoluble differentiation' between the two fields" allowing "each discipline to define its own boundaries, to secure its own self-defined integrity, to proceed with the investigation of its own subject matter according to the methods that are appropriate to the discipline." Any such proposal must also "allow for the possibility of their

Integrating Psychology, Theology, and Spirituality 35

"inseparable unity" from a theological point of view, for in practice "a theological or spiritual perspective cannot always be neatly separated from psychological considerations or vice-versa." Finally, any such proposal must "recognize and appreciate the 'indestructible order' between the two disciplines," acknowledging "that a certain asymmetry exists between them by virtue of their respective subject matters existing on different levels." Therefore, any such proposal must observe "how the psychological concepts are properly understood within a larger theological frame of reference rather than the reverse." Any such proposal must recognize "that there are no sources in the current document. The two sets of concepts cannot be systematically correlated with one another," because any such correlation would suggest that they exist on the same level.

It should be emphasized that by adapting Barth's reasoning, especially his notion of asymmetry, Hunsinger precludes viewing the language of each discipline as interchangeable, thereby reducing the effectiveness of bilingual counseling. She explains that taken by itself, the idea of being "bilingual" would imply a situation of "symmetry" because two different languages like French and English can be thought of as being materially equivalent to one another so that in general one can translate freely back and forth between them without any loss in meaning. Citing the stipulation of asymmetry and its implications, she argues that "no such material equivalence exists between theology and psychology, for their essential subject matters are fundamentally different." Therefore she cautions that even though a counselor is competent in both fields of discourse, care should be taken "not to translate theological into psychological categories or vice versa," especially since "theological and psychological modes of discourse are conceived as existing on different levels." But even if areas of overlap are present "only analogies not equivalences can be drawn between them."

Oden (1966, 15–20), in his book, *Kerygma and Counseling: Toward A Covenant Ontology for Secular Psychotherapy*, pursues the question, "In what sense is the psychotherapeutic process analogous to the self-disclosure of God?" "How," he asks, "is a psychotherapy of human self-disclosure related to a theology of divine self-disclosure? How does the kerygma illuminate the counseling process?" Specifically, he asks, "Can a humanistic therapy and a theology of revelation be meaningfully and self-consistently conjoined in a single ministry of preaching and counseling?" He explains that we are pressed to ask ourselves: "How can a therapy which assumes that man has within himself the capacity for appropriate self-direction provided he has a safe context in which to explore his feelings be consistent with a theology which assumes that the possibility for authentic existence comes to man as a gift mediated once for all through the self-disclosure of God in Jesus Christ?"

Oden (43) contends that humanistic therapy and a theology of revelation can conditionally be meaningfully and self-consistently conjoined in a single ministry of preaching and counseling. He elaborates: "If genuine therapeutic growth is based upon human self-disclosure, as Jourard's thesis suggests, and, if authentic human self-disclosure exists as a response to divine revelation, as the kerygma suggests, then, the divine self-disclosure is properly the precondition of authentic psychotherapeutic growth." Elaborating he emphasizes that "an adequate theory of therapy must not only understand therapeutic growth as a product of human self-disclosure, but authentic human self-disclosure as a response to the self-disclosure of God in being itself."

Oden (81–82) argues that "the psychotherapeutic process, although distinct from revelation, implicitly presupposes an ontological assumption" that enables "by means of the analogy of faith," to identify "christologically the so-called secular counseling situation as the arena of God's self-disclosure." Oden elaborates, "If the self is understood, by definition, as unavoidably standing in relation to the One who gives it life, then understanding of oneself must in some sense be an understanding of that ultimate reality which is the ground and source of selfhood." He cautions that "this does not mean that self-understanding is synonymous with the divine self-disclosure, since revelation differs from insight in that the initiative for it comes from another," but the "Other who speaks in authentic insight is spoken of in the witness of the Christian community." For "revelation is related to insight as speaking is to hearing, however inadequately the hearer may know of the nature of the reality speaking to him in his insight into himself."

Oden (162–63) concludes therefore that "all psychotherapy embodies an expectation for deliverance analogous to the Christ hopes of the Judeo-Christian tradition." For all psychotherapies ultimately reveal a quest for the Christ as an "extricable ingredient." They all imply an "expectation of deliverance from human bondage." Oden explains that if one is still waiting for meaning to be revealed in their life, they are still waiting for Christ. Is Jesus the Christ? This "remains a question for decision in every context, not the least of which is the psychotherapeutic relationship." But to affirm that Jesus is the Christ, Oden (170) emphasizes, "is to affirm that the reality which we meet in the *now* is the reconciling, forgiving, renewing reality which is proclaimed and celebrated in the therapeutic ministry of Jesus of Nazareth. Thus if psychotherapy exists in quest for the Christ, the *kerygma* announces the end of all our Christ quests."

Oden (83) also notes that it is possible for theologians "to take a phenomenological view of the process of psychotherapy." For example, the psychology of Carl Rogers can be interpreted in theological terms viewing his entire work "as a kind of demythologized or perhaps dekerygmatized theology." Rogers can be readily understood within the systematic theology frameworks of sin humanities predicament, grace deliverance from the predicament, and authenticity maturity and self-fulfillment. Therefore Roger's notions of "incongruence, introjected values, and conditions of worth" are analogous to the human predicament of sin. "Empathy, congruence, unconditional positive regard" become synonymous with expressions of redemption or God's grace. "Openness to experience, congruence, and the fully functioning person" incorporate the notion of authenticity or "growth in grace" (109).

Oden (109–13) is quick to point out, however, that whereas Rogers's terms are analogous to classical Protestant theological notions, they do not necessarily convey the same meaning. For example, Rogers "develops a soteriology without a Christology . . . a humanistic soteriology without any acknowledged celebration of God's act, God's acceptance, God's unconditional positive regard." Oden elaborates: "Rogers's theology is a restricted humanism, which in the last analysis is a kind of dehumanization." Rogers's "fails to see man in his deepest dimension as under God, and exaggerates the human capacity for ultimate self-fulfillment apart from God's own delivering activity." He presents man "as a gifted and estranged creature" but fails "to perceive man in the profound dimension of his being created, claimed, and judged by God." Redemption for Rogers "is narrowly limited to personal self-reconciliation of society or a broader hope for the redemption of the cosmos." His view of growth toward authenticity, Oden contends, "lacks a fuller perception of human wholeness illuminated by the divine wholeness, a deeper full-functioning enriched by God's own gracious functioning." Therefore, Oden concludes, "What we have called a 'saving event' in Rogers's theology is, according to Christian wisdom, not a saving event at all in the fullest sense, if the ultimate redemption of human history is finally in God's hands." Oden further explains that "Rogers's concept of introjected values tends toward antinomianism . . . toward a blanket rejection of legitimate means of social control, ignoring the validity of moral constructs and external demands in the growth of personal freedom toward a mature conscience and social responsibility." Rogers's quasi-theology also neglects any concept of authentic human community. For as Oden's understanding of traditional Christian wisdom reveals, "if genuine healing is to take place in the estranged man, he stands in dire need of a nurturing, disciplining, supportive community which would mediate to him the means of grace by which to feed and enable his freedom to love and serve in the midst of human alienation."

Oden (1984), in a book entitled, *Care of Souls in the Classical Tradition*, revisits many of his previous concerns as he once again questions whether the Christian proclamation of unmerited grace can be "made consistent with humanistic-Socratic counseling" (20). Oden proceeds to make a passionate plea for the return to classical models of pastoral care as represented by the likes of Cyprian, Tertullian, Chrysostom, Augustine, Gregory, Luther, Calvin, Herbert, Baxter, and Taylor. He cites compelling evidence that twentieth century pastoral writers such as Hiltner, Clinebell, Oates, Wise, Tournier, Stolberg, and Nuten make no reference to classical texts of pastoral care but instead frequently reference modern psychotherapies as presented by Freud, Jung, Rogers, Fromm, Sullivan, and Berne (30–31). Fearing that modern psychotherapies have usurped the classical tradition of pastoral care, Oden vehemently argues that "a major effort is needed to rediscover and re-mine the classical models of Christian pastoral care" (26).

Oden further explains that a revitalization of the classical models hold the promise of an "enriched synthesis" between the classical models and modern psychotherapy. Oden (37) explains that "the task that lies ahead is the development of a postmodern, post-Freudian, neoclassical approach to Christian pastoral care that takes seriously the resources of modernity while also penetrating its illusions." Oden argues that we should keep in mind the problems that modern psychotherapies present, especially when classical tradition serve as our bearings, yet not discounting lessons learned from modern clinical experience.

Oden (37–40) argues that such an enterprise will require "intelligent resistance to the narcissistic imperialism and hedonistic reductionism that prevail both in the culture and, to a large extent, in the churches." Such an undertaking would require the "reconstruction of a pastoral care that is informed by Christian theology." This would result in a pastoral care that incorporates the use of intercessory prayer, combats antinomianism, upholds the doctrine of holy matrimony, and includes "empathy training" that is "grounded in an incarnational understanding of God's participation in human alienation." It would result in a pastoral care that emphasizes Christian anthropology, reintroduces "corporate responsibility, mutual accountability, moral self-examination, and social commitment," and advocates the return to the study of Scripture and Christian tradition. Evangelical witnessing would once again be part of the therapeutic dialogue. This would result in a pastoral counseling that once again is "an integral part of the pastoral office intrinsically correlated with liturgy, preaching, and the nurture of the Christian community, and relatively less identified with purely secularized, non-ecclesial, theologically emasculated, fee-basis counseling."

Browning (1987, xi–17), in his book, *Religious Thought and the Modern Psychotherapies: A Critical Conversation in the Theology of Culture*, is careful to distinguish between psychology as "a relatively objective and scientific discipline dedicated to the development of a body of knowledge about the patterns in human symbolic and behavioral activity" and a view of psychology "which conceives psychology as a practical discipline based on a critical ethic and a critical theory of society." Browning further elaborates that "scientific psychologies claim to have a more rigorous relation to highly specifiable orders of concrete data than is the case with the philosophical psychologies." The practice of clinical psychology, Browning contends, mirrors more a philosophical psychology. Although the clinical psychologies "want their concepts to 'fit' or 'account' for certain observations they make in the clinical settings," they do not "achieve prediction or repeatability as do the experimentalists." Their notions, unlike the experimental psychologies, are not fully derived from controlled observations so that "variables can be isolated, cause or correlations statistically stated, and publicly repeatable verification achieved." For example, the likes of "Freud, Jung, Erikson, Kohut, and the humanistic psychologists Carl Rogers, Abraham Maslow, and Fritz Perls are largely clinical psychologists, whereas B. F. Skinner is clearly an experimental psychologist."

Browning claims that after clinical philosophical psychology has been clearly distinguished from experimental scientific psychology, at least four cultures of contemporary psychology remain: the culture of detachment, the culture of joy, the culture of control, and the culture of care. Browning presents these cultures in light of his overriding investigative theme of examining "the potential relationships between two sources of modern individual identity—religious faith as it has been formed by the Judeo-Christian tradition of the West and the disciplines of psychology as these have developed in the twentieth century." Browning argues that such an investigation is warranted because "traditional religion and modern psychology stand in a special relation to one another, because both of them provide concepts and technologies for the ordering of the interior life." Browning's inquiry focuses on an overarching question. Will our culture be "oriented and directed by our inherited religious traditions or will it increasingly gain its orientation, especially with regard to the inner life, from the modern psychologies?" Furthermore, are the two compatible? Is there a way "to state the appropriate relationship between these two perspectives thereby giving each its proper space?" Browning asks: "How do individuals who have been taught to orient their lives around the wisdom of Judeo-Christian religious thought handle the social sciences, especially the psychologies? How do they read these psychologies, understand what knowledge they give us, comprehend their boundaries, and most importantly of all, discern both their limits and what they cannot, do not, or should not tell us or claim to tell us?"

Browning explains that historically, Christianity has been variously affected by the philosophies of the "Stoic, neo-Platonic, Aristotelian, Thomistic, Hegelian, Kierkegaardian, Heideggerian, and Whiteheadian psychologies." These philosophical psychologies were more than "hatched up, or imagined, or mere products of speculative reason," but accounted for "rather wide ranges of human experience—so wide, in fact, that they do not easily fit within the confines of rigorous experimental procedures or the narrow focus of behavioral or affective problems associated with the clinic." Similarly, Browning argues, modern twentieth-century psychologies, by means of their impact on the symbols and norms that guide a society and their impact on culture, have developed "religio-ethical dimensions" that entitle them to be challenged as any other philosophical psychology. Browning explains: "If these different psychologies were strictly psychologies, Christian thought would have little to say about them. But insofar as these psychologies give rise to cultures with genuine religio-ethical dimensions, Christian thought is entitled to engage them in critical conversation." For in reality, twentieth-century clinical psychology has moved beyond the narrow confines of a rigorous science and now infringes on the theological task of orienting "the believer to the broadest ranges of human experience, to describe and represent what experience testifies to be its ultimate context, and to induce the appropriate existential and ethical response." Browning explains: "The clinical psychologies, on the other hand, stand somewhere between experimental psychology and theology; rather than prediction and control based on the manipulation of discrete facts of sense experience, the clinical psychologies—or at least some of them—are thought to be concerned with the interpretation of basic patterns, modalities, themes, and narratives which give lives their underlying cohesion."

Browning elaborates that what was once left up to systematic Christian theology, "the specific sense of taking basic questions about the meaning of human existence that each cultural expression characteristically asks and correlating them with the answer provided by Christian revelation," is now being usurped by the renderings of modern clinical psychology. But in doing so, Browning argues, clinical psychology has moved beyond its scope of inquiry, beyond describing "the tensions and ambiguities of existence in the language, symbols, and forms of a particular era and a particular region of experience," to attempting to give "answers to the basic problems of existence" and to this extent, psychology begins to compete with theology.

Critical to the understanding of Browning's presentation is his bold assertion that there are "metaphorical underpinnings" in both science and theology. Citing the work of Lakoff and Johnson (1980), Browning emphasizes that metaphorical language is especially evident in theology and psychology. Browning defines metaphor as "understanding and experiencing one kind of thing in terms of another" that enables one to link "the known to the unknown" by selectively transferring "the familiar associations of a word to the new context." Browning points out that metaphor help us "investigate the unknown" and "talk about the unfamiliar," especially when religious discernment and scientific discovery are involved. Browning explains: "We represent our sense of the holy in terms of metaphors, but through metaphors we also probe with our imaginations the unknown realms of nature in our effort scientifically to represent its otherwise unfathomable reaches" (19). Browning concludes, therefore, that "it is not only in theology but, to a surprising extent, in the modern psychologies as well that the way we metaphorically represent the world in its most durable and ultimate respects influences although not necessarily determines in all respects what we think we are obligated to do" (20).

Browning bolsters his position when he shows how "Freud's early use of mechanistic metaphors and his later use of the metaphors of life and death imply a particular view of life," setting "the stage for what he thought was ethically possible for humans to achieve, that is, a modest and cautious degree of reciprocity that would not overtax our limited libidinal investments or arouse our ready hostilities."

Therefore Freud introduces the metaphor of *civilized detachment* into the culture.

Browning further strengthens his argument by showing how "humanistic psychology's implicit metaphors of harmony" introduce a metaphor of *expressive joy* into the culture. This *expressive joy* is evidenced when we remain true to our deepest selves, true to our inner plan for self-actualization. His argument is also enhanced when he shows how Skinner introduces the metaphor of *ultimacy* into the culture that "build's around the Darwinian doctrine of natural selection and what it implies for the selective and reinforcing power of the environment." Total justice, not self-actualization, "was Skinner's implicit ethic, and the selecting, reinforcing, and controlling powers of the environment should be enlisted to bring such a justice into reality."

His position is further validated as he outlines how Jung introduces a metaphor of *archetypes*, a kind of "sacred egoism" which "will lead to a deeper harmony because of the final complementarities between each person's archetypal possibilities and the structure of the world."

Final fortification of Browning's position is provided by Erikson and Kohut, as Browning shows how these psychologists introduce a metaphor of *generative care* into the culture—an ethic and culture of care built around a model that sees health as "the capacity for generative care for succeeding generations," where the "self-actualization motif of the humanistic psychologies" is not only maintained, but is also transformed "by seeing the generative care of others as also an avenue for the actualization of each human's own deepest inclinations" (30–31).

Collectively, the introduction of metaphors by modern psychology, especially the metaphors of joy, ultimacy in the form of total justice, archetypes, and generative care, help shore up Browning's conclusion that the modern psychologies, with "their ideas and wider horizons, seriously as an independent source of culture" deserve "appreciative and critical evaluation from another source of culture—traditional anthropologies shaped by elements of the Jewish and Christian religious traditions" (31). Browning recognizes that "no psychology, and especially no clinical or psychotherapeutic psychology, can ever completely eliminate its implicit metaphors of ultimacy and moral images." It can, however, "attempt to be aware of them and name them for what they are without invoking for them the authority of science." Furthermore, psychology "can then submit these moral and metaphysical horizons to philosophical testing insofar as they appear necessary to orient psychology to the world of praxis" (60).

In summary, Browning's careful scrutiny of several modern psychotherapies has led him to conclude that "whatever the differences between these new psychologies and the Judeo-Christian tradition it cannot be that the psychologies are without metaphors of ultimacy and principles of obligation." In fact what we have witnessed is "a subtle process of psychology gradually becoming both religion and ethics" (89). Indeed modern psychologies can be treated "more as systems of practical moral philosophy than as simply scientific or clinical psychologies." Conceding that modern psychologies do make "genuinely valid scientific statements and clinical values," nonetheless "they are not only or strictly scientific in either the clinical or experimental sense of the term." Instead, they consistently reflect "moral and metaphorical overtones" as they focus on the question of cure and healing (238). Furthermore, the metaphors of modern psychologies have become "deeply embedded in the social forces of modern life" becoming an "ideological expression of and tool for these social contextual patterns," becoming "responses to the forces of modern capitalist societies of a religio-ethical kind." And in many ways their religio-ethical responses are "on the same logical level as the inherited Judeo-Christian responses." Therefore, Browning argues, "they are entirely respectable candidates for the exercise in a critical theology of culture" (238–42). In that modern psychologies are normative in their definitions, they "must do their research in close association with the normative disciplines of ethics, political science, and . . . theology." Browning explains: "Hence, our psychologies as well as our other social sciences must be critical psychologies." Our psychologies "should be disciplines that self-consciously mix descriptive and experimental work with normative work about the nature of the good person and the good society and their dialectical relation" (242–43). Modern psychologies, therefore, are "not so much wrong in principle as unreflective, naïve, and philosophically and ethically immature if not downright dangerous." Therefore, psychologies "should not rid themselves of deep metaphors," but instead should strive to base their psychologies "on better and more critically grounded dimensions of practical thought . . . from the perspective of their metaphysical as well as their moral adequacy." Psychologies should understand that such "critically grounded dimensions" can be provided by religion and theology (244).

Thurneysen (1962, 200–20) contends that pastoral counseling "needs psychology as an auxiliary science which serves to examine man's inner being," but the pastoral counselor must be careful to dissociate oneself "from the essential alien philosophical presuppositions inherent in psychology," assumptions which could impair one's "understanding of man derived from Holy Scripture." Thurneysen emphasizes that the true task of pastoral care involves the "inner life of man as the soil where the guiding Word takes root"; nonetheless, pastoral care "needs psychology as its outstanding auxiliary." But Thurneysen points out that "pastoral care is a discipline of its own, interchangeably distinct and different from psychology and psychotherapy." Thurneysen explains:

> "Pastoral care is and remains proclamation of the Word to the individual and neither can nor should ever be anything else. But—and here begins the relationship between pastoral care and psychology—in order to deliver the Word of forgiveness to man, we must avail ourselves of a knowledge of his inner life in as exact, methodical, and comprehensive a way as is possible. Without such knowledge, our talk with him cannot possibly lead to deliverance, its goal."

Thurneysen concludes therefore, that although "we assert the primacy of Holy Scripture over psychology and its knowledge of human nature," understanding that the Word of God is "the basis of all knowledge even in the matter of understanding man," this in no way "belittles psychology and its research." For the pastoral counselor, "our use of psychological findings only serves to elucidate the understanding of man given us in the Word of God."

Collins (1988, 128–30) raises the question as to whether psychology can be trusted. Is psychology anti-Christian? Does it dabble in the demonic? Should non-Christian counselors be avoided? Does psychology really work? For at the core of Collins's questions is whether or not secular psychology and Christianity can be integrated. He concludes that to date scholarly inquiry has shown that "Christians and psychologists can learn from each other, without weakening or watering down the enduring truths of God's Word." These intellectual exchanges "can be done without weakening the spiritual commitment of the searcher who accepts God's Word and learns from the study of God's creation." The question still remains as to whether "psychology and Christianity can be integrated, but for too many sincere believers, the future of this endeavor looks promising."

Collins, therefore, seems committed to the intellectual challenge of integrating the two disciplines, but cautions that some parts of psychology cannot be integrated, especially when the psychological propositions proposed clearly violate Scripture. But he clarifies that sometimes integration is unavoidable. Arguing that life is never simple, Collins points out that dichotomizing counseling into psychological versus the biblical approach overlooks reality. For example, both approaches require "listening, talking, confessing, accepting, thinking, and understanding," and both confront such concepts as "love, hope, compassion, forgiveness, caring, and kindness."

Narramore (1997, 6–10) asserts that when attempting to integrate psychology with theology one needs to be "aware of and sophisticated about the philosophical presuppositions, e.g., naturalism, positivism, relativism, individuality, and secularity undergirding most of the work in the discipline of psychology and the implications of those presuppositions for integrative theorizing." In addition, such integration must take place "within a well-defined biblical-Christian worldview." Moreover, such integration requires "exploring new content areas in their efforts to integrate psychology with Christian beliefs and practice," while delving "into various secular theoretical perspectives in order to carry out both a more thorough critique and to seek more sophisticated levels of understanding within which to apply their integrative work." This will enable Christian psychologists "to relate careful integrative theorizing to the clinical work of psychotherapists and counselors."

Johnson (1997, 11–27) emphasizes the importance of remembering that the "lordship of Christ over all of a Christian's life" must be our starting assumption in any attempt to integrate psychology with Christian theology. Recognizing how problematic this will be, "because of the pervasive naturalism and neo-positivism of modern psychology," and the influence on psychology "by unbelieving individuals . . . and their underlying anti-spiritual agenda," he reminds us that we are still "called to work towards the expression of Christ's lordship in psychology."

Johnson's exploration of how the lordship of Christ relates to psychology leads him to conclude that psychology "is not an independent activity that operates apart from God." Instead, it is "dependent upon God's mercy to illuminate human understanding and reveal things about human nature through human reflection, research, and creative insight." Johnson emphasizes that "empirical methods can reveal the consequences of certain conditions or behaviors," but these methods "cannot clearly tell people how to evaluate those consequences." Nor can psychology "provide transcultural criteria for human maturity and mental health." Although psychology "inevitably assumes some normative goals regarding human nature," because "God's mind includes what people should be, science and therapy should be informed by God's understanding of the human *telos*, and not simply human nature as it is."

Therefore, for Johnson, deciding whether to integrate psychological concepts into Christian counseling involves at least five steps. The psychological concept must first be evaluated within the context of "one's Christian evaluative framework," thereby avoiding "a ghetto in one's minds" that would provide "no evaluative influence on the secular material one reads." Secondly, an attempt must be made "to understand the finding or concept that is the focus of integration." Next, the finding or concept "should be assessed in terms of its compatibility with the Scriptures as well as whether it meets other validity criteria, including theoretic support, statistical procedures, research design, sampling, empirical evidence, and so forth." If the concept passes this standard, then the "degree of theoretical complexity and, correspondingly, the level of integration that is involved will need to be assessed." Finally, if the concept passes the prior tests, "the task of Christian translation or reconceptualization follows. This step entails "making a sense of the original finding or concept according to a Christian evaluative framework and grammar."

Johnson concludes his discourse by reemphasizing "two of the most important issues in human life: who shall be Lord and how shall one change into his likeness? Conceding that "all perspectives on human nature are important," Johnson argues that "some are more important than others . . . especially the religious dimensions." He explains: "Biological and behavioral findings need to be interpreted within a larger person-centered framework that recognizes human choice and responsibility, and this framework, in turn, should be interpreted within a theocentric framework in which all humans are understood before God." Involving a theocentric framework within the counseling process may uncover the client's difficulties as "a function of the pathology of their values." Therefore, in such cases, "the best thing the kingdom-minded counselor could do would be to help them to find better values: the values of the kingdom" (25).

Monroe (1997, 28–37) identifies four tension areas between psychology and theology: "the role of the Bible in creating a comprehensive anthropology and theory of human behavior, sin and human behavior, the spiritual nature of life, and the purpose of counseling." Monroe contends that the integration of psychology and theology will necessitate fully exploring "how the biblical data impact and fill out our understanding of human motivation and behavior." It will also require "a discussion of sin and its relation to human behavior." For example, he questions: "What are the varying effects of being both sinner and sinned against? Are victims of sinful behavior also responsible for their response to that sin? If so, how do we appropriately describe it?" Also, "Does our understanding of sin encompass not only willful sin but that of lifestyle, or blind, idolatrous, sin?" Or, "How does our conception of sin affect our understanding of mental well-being? More important, "Are psychologists prepared to accurately identify sinful thinking, feeling, and doing and handle it appropriately?"

The discussion must also encompass "the spiritual nature of life . . . as it relates to the issue of spiritual versus psychological problems." For example: "Does every mental health problem have a spiritual component?" Or "is it just a component or does it permeate every aspect of mental health?" Do we make a distinction between idolatry and addiction? Do we treat a psychological problem such as panic without dealing openly with spiritual problems? "How does our understanding that every thought, behavior, or feeling has a Godward referent affect our understanding of psychological problems?"

The discussion must also embrace "the ultimate purpose of counseling." Should counseling ultimately focus on the "eternal perspective of the relationship between people and God" or simply be content in "helping to remove barriers" that would keep one from an emotionally satisfying life? Should the counselor's focus be limited to "the problems of everyday life," or should the focus attempt to define one's "dysfunctional relationship with God?" Moreover, "How does the ultimate meaning of human problems affect how we deal with them on a temporal level? Is the purpose of counseling merely horizontal dealing with human relationships or vertical dealing with our relationship with God? Is it both? Is one purpose more primary than another?"

Clouse (1997, 38–48) explores the question of whether psychology and theology can be linked. Clouse explains, for example, that "the concept of sin in Christian theology resembles the psychoanalytic view of irrational passions and instincts insofar as sin is wanting one's way and caring for self more than for others," but a Christian understanding of "sin goes well beyond the psychoanalytic understanding of depravity." For the Christian, "The purpose of life is more than an ego coping with a real world," for it involves "a meaningful relationship with the Creator and Redeemer." For the Christian, life is more than "unconscious processes, psychic determinism, mechanistic forces, and instinctual drives," but instead the Christian life embraces "the conscious or rational component of one's being, free will and self-determination, goals and purposes, and religious or moral forces." For "well-being in Christianity is more than a regrouping of forces already present within the personality." It involves God's grace and becoming "a new creation in Christ Jesus." Whereas the Christian life embraces "a divine Creator and Redeemer," for Freud and psychoanalysis "there is no salvation apart from what the person can do to free the self from an irrational id and an overdemanding superego. Apart from temporary relief from neurotic tension, Freud's views lack the hope and promise offered by "an all-powerful and all-loving God" who "has chosen to free people from the bondage of sin."

Clouse asks: "Can learning psychology and Christianity walk together?" Clouse concludes: "The technology of learning psychology becomes an informative source to help people understand themselves and others; and by being knowledgeable of the methods and applying them appropriately, people can enhance God's plan in the lives of those entrusted to their care," but much of the philosophy of learning psychology "is incompatible with Christian belief."

Clouse asks: "Can cognitive psychology and Christianity walk together? Are the two compatible?" Clouse does find some links between cognitive psychology and the Scriptures, especially centering on the notions of rationality, justice, and joy. Furthermore, he reports that for the most part, those attempting to integrate cognitive principles into clinical practice find their underlying assumptions neither "endearing nor offensive."

Clouse asks, "Can humanistic psychology and Christianity walk together?" He concludes yes, if humanistic psychology refers to "what Packer and Howard (1985) called *sacred humanism*." Contending that humanism belongs to Christianity in the first place, Clouse (54) explains, "Sacred humanism sees Jesus Christ as the standard of humanness; secular humanism has "no Creator to worship, no Redeemer to love . . . no heavenly glory to inherit" (13). In another source, Packer (1978) states, "I am a humanist. In truth, I believe it is only a thoroughgoing Christian who can ever have a right to that name. . . . It is part of the glory of the gospel to be the one genuine humanism that the world has seen" (11). MacKay (1979) echoes this sentiment by writing, "Christian humanism affirms that the only true fulfillment is to be found in working out our destiny in line with the will of our Creator" (109). Brown (1970) puts it this way: "Christianity at its best does not oppose humanism: rather, Christianity is humanism plus."

But secular humanism, in contrast, is diametrically opposed to sacred humanism. "This life is all we have," argues the secular humanist. Thought and action, therefore, are purposeful to the extent that they enhance "earthly human interests on behalf of the greater happiness and glory of man," never experiencing self-denial, "but rather an enhancement and affirmation of one's identity . . . to be self-actualized." Denouncing a need for God, humanity itself assumes godlike qualities.

In summarizing, Clouse concludes that the compatibility between psychology and theology is "harmonic and discordant, sometimes agreeing and sometimes not" with "each of the major theories in psychology: psychoanalysis, learning psychology behaviorism, cognitive psychology, and humanism" finding "support from Scripture." Likewise, "Each has elements that are in opposition to what the Bible teaches." However, he emphasizes, whereas the Christian counselor "may have to reject the philosophical assumptions of a psychology," the Christian counselor may still use "the methodology to further the work of Christian ministry."

Brokaw (1997, 81–85) cites several references that have attempted to outline "the difference between psychologically constructive versus defensive use of prayer, Scripture, or religious dialogue in therapy, by clients or therapists." She also reports that the examination of the "impact of internalized relationships on one's relationship with God is increasingly being explored. Important therapeutic issues "such as shame, guilt, and forgiveness, are being further considered in relation to various types of pathology and character structures." In addition, she reports "a renewed interest in the practice of spiritual disciplines, including contemplative prayer, solitude, and biblical meditation."

Hall and Hall (1997, 86–101) provide an overview of attempts that have been made to incorporate religious values and beliefs into traditional psychological frameworks and the spectrum of this integration. They conclude that there is ample evidence supporting a need for clinical integration, that there is a spectrum of thought about the nature of such integration, and that any such integration raises some ethical issues. Hall and Hall cite evidence that suggests incorporating religious content more systematically into psychotherapy will contribute "to one's understanding of human nature by acknowledging that there is a spiritual reality and that spiritual experiences make a difference in human behavior." This, they explain, will enable the therapist to help the counselee explore the "laws and principles" that guide their spiritual system. Furthermore, "a spiritual perspective helps the therapist and the counselee "anchor values in universal terms," thereby fostering "the goals of treatment, the selection of techniques, and the evaluation of outcomes." Introduction of a spiritual perspective also enables the therapist to incorporate into the counseling process a broader "range of techniques, including intrapsychic methods such as prayer, rituals, and Scripture study, as well as community resources such as communal spiritual experiences."

Hall and Hall report that integration is justified because "a significant proportion of the populations seem to prefer religiously-sensitive psychotherapy, and religious material may be unavoidable in therapy." They explain: "The persistence and pervasiveness of religious concerns and moral values is an indication that this is an important area for most people. In addition, psychotherapy and religion overlap in their scope of concern with regard to the meaning of life and moral values." They also explain that the ethical considerations surrounding multiculturalism demand the incorporation of religious content. They emphasize that "religion is not only an important variable in human diversity," but religious beliefs and values "are an important motivational force in many religiously-committed clients." Not to consider religious content, they conclude, places the therapist "in danger of acting unethically by imposing his or her values without the client's consent" and "shows a lack of respect both for the client's value system and for the social system represented by the value system." Furthermore, excluding religious content may exclude more effective approaches than traditional psychotherapy can provide.

McMinn and McRay (1997, 102–10) stress the importance of spiritual practices as an important factor in the integration of psychology and Christianity. However, they note that "there has been little discussion of the relationship of psychology with spiritual practices such as the Christian disciplines of prayer, meditation, fasting, solitude, service, confession, and worship." But they are quick to point out that the "Christian understanding of health" often significantly clashes with psychological notions of mental health, especially since "Christian discipline has historically been rooted in the authority of Scripture and faith practices whereas the epistemological roots of contemporary professional psychology are predominantly based on science and personality theory." Subsequently, "differing epistemological foundations have led to distinct, and sometimes conflicting, ways of understanding health and healing." They explain: "In this evangelical Christian worldview, an awareness of personal need and brokenness is a prerequisite to healing. From this perspective, 'sickness' is not so much a set of symptoms as a part of human nature." The central human problem, they explain, "is much more pervasive than a psychiatric diagnosis can capture, and extends to those who have no psychiatric diagnosis. To enter into health and hope, one must acknowledge that inner peace can never come through personal efforts alone, but only by yielding control of one's life to God." They conclude that at the heart of Christian spirituality "is a healing relationship with God. In the context of this Christian worldview, the spiritual disciplines enable one to move beyond myths of self-sufficiency and experience God's redemptive presence."

Adopting this viewpoint shifts the ultimate goal for therapy to the promotion of Christian character. "Faith and the existential questions associated with it" form the fabric of health. Faith becomes a "psychological and spiritual dynamic which encompasses the totality of being in the Christian life" being "at the very heart of the human epistemological crisis, causing people to be utterly dependent upon God who sustains all that is real."

Bufford (1997, 115–18) argues that Christian and non-Christian approaches share several factors in common. For one, both usually address similar types of problems: "depression, anxiety, relationship conflicts, addictions, and so on." Both also show an interest in spirituality. Furthermore, many theories of Christian counseling "have been adopted or adapted from existing counseling theories" or bear striking resemblances to them. In addition, "intervention strategies and techniques are largely common among Christian and non-Christian approaches." Bufford concludes that "while goals such as discipleship and spiritual maturity clearly are distinctive," the "more immediate goals, such as alleviation of depressive symptoms, reduction of anxiety, management of anger, self-discipline, or control over addictions, are common in both Christian and non-Christian approaches despite the underlying differences in worldview and values."

Bridger and Atkinson (1998, 41–52) outline four positions often expounded when answering the question "Are theology and psychology to be regarded as friends or enemies?"[2] Citing Kirwan (1984), they explain that one school of thought, the "un-Christian view," claims that "theology has nothing to contribute to therapy . . . the two disciplines have nothing to say to each other." At best, theology is "an irrelevance . . . it might even be a factor in producing a patients neurosis." Freud and material reductionists such as Albert Ellis and B. F. Skinner would argue such a view.

Another position often asserted, the spiritualized view, emphatically denies "that psychology has any value in comparison with religion. Theology is all that is needed. Psychology is rendered unnecessary by grace: "the Holy Spirit is the great psychiatrist." Adams (1970), Bobgan and Bobgan (1979), and Powlison (1992) would be representative of this point of view.

Yet another viewpoint, the parallel view, contends "that psychology and theology are equally valid within their respective spheres but their authority is confined to those spheres." "Each functions sovereignly but independently," being incapable of deriding the other "since both are dealing with separate realities." Hunsinger (1995) would most likely come close to advocating this position.

2. Note, as do Carter and Narramore (1979), the similarities to H. Richard Niebuhr's (1951) attempt to explicate the relationship between Christian theology and culture in *Christ and Culture*.

Still others argue for the integrated view. This position claims "that there is no sphere of sovereignty in the psychological-theological relationship." When "each is rightly understood, there is no inherent conflict . . . representing functionally cooperative positions." Collins (1988), Oden (1966), and Lake (1966) would be representative examples of this position.

Bridger and Atkinson make clear that there is a "continuum of responses" to the questions of compatibility between psychology and theology ranging from "outright hostility between theology through compartmentalized co-existence to complimentarity and final assimilation." Bridger and Atkinson quickly reject any attempts to "reduce either psychology or theology to each other" and instead embrace Farnsworth's (1985) notion of critical perspectivalism—"that any phenomena can be described at different levels or from different perspectives according to the discipline that is asking the questions." Defending their conclusion, they maintain that this "is the only approach which respects the integrity both of individual disciplines and truth as a whole." Furthermore, it asserts the belief "that although our perspectives on truth may be limited, partial, and provisional, all truth is nevertheless God's truth and that integration between theology and psychology is concerned with precisely that."

Farnsworth and Regier (1997, 155–63) address a practical question when they ask: "How much psychology and how much theology should one incorporate into Christian counseling?" They conclude: "Those Christian counselors adopt the practical and helpful distinction made by Browning (1987) that (a) theology's domain is ultimate meaning and moral obligation, and (b) psychology's domain is personal needs and developmental tendencies." A revision is proposed, therefore, to read theology in its "primary domain" and psychology in its "only domain." What we have then is a distinction that says psychology operates at the level of description, analysis, and treatment of human needs and tendencies—the problems that bring hurting people to counseling and their strengths and weaknesses that must be incorporated into treatment."

They point out that theology "functions most appropriately at the level of providing prescriptions for the spiritually meaningful and morally organized expression of our needs and tendencies." For example, psychology provides us with many details regarding human sexuality, but it is "our biblical theology of obligation and ultimacy that directs its expression as moral and meaningful."

They conclude, therefore, that the clinician should only draw on psychology "for the description, analysis, and treatment of human needs and tendencies, and utilize biblical theology primarily for directing one's actions in ways that are spiritually meaningful and moral."

Jones (1996, 113–47) examines the commonalities and distinctions between religion and science. He concludes that each discipline "grapples with real aspects of human experience." But whereas science is more likely "to deal with the more sensory, objective, public, quantifiable, and repeatable aspects of experience," religion is more apt "to deal with the more internal, subjective, qualitative, and un-measurable aspects of human experience . . . with the nature of the transcendent through revelation, reason, and human experience."

Jones emphasizes, however, that there "is a certain degree of uncertainty and interpretation involved in all human knowing." "Certainly," he argues, "scientists grapple with the abstract, private, ephemeral, and subjective, especially in psychology." Furthermore, all areas of inquiry "should and do each exhibit a certain epistemic humility and hold themselves open to correction and development, at the same time aiming toward verisimilitude—truth-likeness."

Jones also concludes that religion and science both attempt to make sense out of a very complex existence. Jones explains that "scientific explanations are distinguished by their emphasis on the development of what are commonly called universal mathematical-quantitative relationships between naturalistic entities, with the specified relationship being assumed to hold universally whenever comparable conditions apply." In comparison, "religious explanations typically resort to more poetic, dogmatic, metaphorical, or rationalistic explanatory mechanisms than do scientific explanations." But despite their distinctive styles of explanation, he stresses that "both attempt to foster human understanding."

Jones also points out that both disciplines make use of analogical models "rooted in paradigms or worldviews to explain experience." In addition, Jones argues both religion and science are human enterprises, "both are human communal and cultural enterprises subject to the same sorts of human influences that affect all of our activities." Consequently, these "finely nuanced activities" are not "readily reducible to a set of methodological rules or conceptual dogmas." Caution therefore should be exercised by both disciplines so as to not embrace extreme conclusions reducing "the determinants of science to social-cultural forces alone" or in understanding religion in terms of "the reductionistic renderings of religion promulgated by Freud, Skinner, and others."

Jones concludes his comparison by accentuating the fact that both disciplines generate passionate devotion. He explains: "Science can in fact elicit and inspire the same type of passionate devotion as religion can." Elaborating he points out that "human beings seem to be drawn with religious reverence to some ultimate reality, and certainly science occupies that place in the life of many scientists." Indeed, he concludes that "the scientific enterprise is sustained by the emotional commitment of its practitioners to both the grand aims of the pursuit of truth and the improvement of the human race, as well as by the more pedestrian dreams of personal advancement, prestige, and prosperity."

Jones makes it clear in his discussions that it is "inevitable that psychotherapy will be a moral enterprise with substantial interrelationship with broad religious understandings . . . that what many regard to be religious presuppositions are intrinsic to the nature of psychotherapeutic and personality theory." He notes the "intractable presence of metaphysical presuppositions in all clinical theory," because psychotherapeutic theories "embody value assumptions in that each includes explicit or implicit judgments about the nature of the human life that is "good" (healthy, whole, adaptive, realistic, rational, etc.) and "bad" (abnormal, pathological, immature, stunted, self-deceived, etc.)." Therefore, Jones concludes that if "psychological research and practice are going to be maximally effective in understanding and improving the human condition, psychologists would be well advised to explicitly explore the connections of their work with the deepest levels of our human commitments."

Pargament (1997, 3–13) examines the relationship between psychology and religion within the context of coping. He explains: "Hardship, suffering, and conflict have been centers of concern for the major religions of the world." Pargament elaborates when he writes, "Within Buddhism, it is believed that existence is first experienced as suffering (*Dukkha*), a term that embodies physical pain and mental anguish, negative changes, and a lack of freedom" (Gard, 1962). Within Judaism, "suffering in the world is explicitly recognized through the commemoration of slavery and oppression and the celebration of freedom. Christianity presents a model of suffering in the world through the crucifixion of Jesus Christ." Therefore, religions of the world "have a deep appreciation for the often painful nature of the human condition . . . every religion offers a way to come to terms with tragedy, suffering, and the most significant issues in life." Religions of the world have been concerned "about suffering and its amelioration for thousands of years." Pargament points out, however, that as a form of practice to help people better cope, psychology is a twentieth-century phenomenon.

Pargament explains that psychology in the twentieth century has become a rival to religion within Western cultures. Religious phenomena "have been redefined as naturalistic," with religion losing "some of its authority as a source of absolute, indisputable meaning." "Subjective personal concern" has been embraced by psychology as it offers a different perspective "of the 'good life' and its own mechanisms for solving problems." Confession becomes psychotherapy. Conversion becomes personal growth. Sins and virtues become ethics. Because psychology has developed parallels to religion "in its rituals, rites of passage, traditions, use of symbols, and charismatic leaders," psychology's theories and practices have come to function like a religion. But, he points out, where religion has stressed the necessity of letting go as a primary coping strategy, recognizing our powerlessness and limitations and seeking help beyond ourselves, psychology, in contrast, has stressed a theme of personal empowerment, tapping our inner resources to better cope with the demands at hand. At issue for Pargament is the compatibility of these seemingly opposing viewpoints.

Pargament concludes that religion can be enriched through the study of psychology and psychology can be enriched through the study of religion. Although science and religion approach the world differently, "their methods may augment rather than detract from each other." He explains that "there is much to be gained from bridging the worldviews and practices embedded in psychological and religious perspectives. Human capacities and human limitations *complement* rather than *contradict* each other." For he contends that "in times of crisis and coping both the possible and the impossible become visible ... the psychology of religion and coping can weave a respect for the possible together with an appreciation for the futile." Bridging the worldviews helps people "take control of what they can in times of stress with a rich religious tradition of helping people accept their limitations and look beyond themselves for assistance in troubling times."

Psychology can assist religion in punching holes into such myths that "religion is simply a form of denial," as evidence can be garnered showing that religion adds "a unique dimension to the coping process," that "it has the potential to help people through their hardest times and it also has the potential to make bad matters worse." Likewise, religion can assist psychology in "stretching itself as science" by better preparing science to examine the most "inscrutable, deeply enigmatic aspects of life." For "the religious world is too large, too diverse, and too complex," Pargament explains, "to be approached by any single scientific method." Science requires a perspective "from the inside and the outside, a willingness to study religion in its social and situational context, and an appreciation for the variety of ways religion can express itself."

SUMMARY

In this chapter, a review of the literature examining the compatibility of psychology with theology and spirituality has been presented. Implications for the counseling process have also been inferred if not stated outright. It can be construed, therefore, that whereas there is an analogous relationship between psychology and theology and spirituality, the latter is ultimate. When psychology moves beyond the penultimate, wrapping itself in metaphorical garb and varnishing itself with quasi-spiritual solutions that focus on the meaning of existence and present prescriptions of obligation, it runs the danger of becoming a quasi-theology dripping with spiritual overtones. What results is a watered-down scientific discipline that conveys blurred meaning of the phenomena it purports to describe. Furthermore, the ensuing conclusions it draws are often discordant with theological and spiritual perspectives. Also, the underlying assumptions of modern psychology with regard to the nature of humanity and its ultimate concerns often differ significantly from traditional Christian understandings of the plight of humanity.

FUEL FOR THOUGHT

1. Why are psychology and theology arguably incompatible disciplines of inquiry?
2. Explain the "Chalcedonian pattern."
3. What issues emerge when you attempt to integrate psychology and theology into a model for Christian counseling?
4. To what degree are psychological principles compatible with theological principles?
5. What spiritual principles should be incorporated in any model of Christian counseling?

6

Evaluating Models of Christian Counseling

IN ORDER to effectively evaluate a model of Christian counseling, at least three potentially interrelated disciplines of inquiry must be examined. These include the *theological underpinnings* of the model, the *psychological dimensions* evident, and the degree or extent that the model assumes a level of *spiritual intelligence*. Scrutinizing these underlying assumptions enables one to determine the logical consistency of a particular model of Christian counseling and to ascertain the efficacy and efficiency of the approach as a legitimate means of counseling. The adage that "our assumptions determine our outcomes" is certainly applicable to this endeavor.

THEOLOGICAL UNDERPINNINGS

The process of exploring the theological underpinnings of a particular model of Christian counseling involves ascertaining to what extent the author presents implicitly or explicitly a(n):[1]

---

1. Definitions used are adapted from the *Westminster Dictionary of Theological Terms* (McKim 1996).

- Doctrine of God—the study of what is believed to be true about God.
- Cosmology—the study of the universe, including its origin, evolution, and overall structure.
- Anthropology—study of the doctrine of humanity, which views humans in terms of their relationship to God. It encompasses reflecting on such issues as the origin, purpose, and destiny of humankind in light of Christian theological understandings.
- Harmartiology—the study of the doctrine of sin.
- Soteriology—the study of the doctrine of salvation.
- Christology—the study of the person and work of Jesus Christ.
- Pneumatology—the study of the theological doctrine of the Holy Spirit.
- Ecclesiology—the study of the church as a biblical and theological topic.
- Eschatology—the study of the last things or the end of the world.

In general, the theological similarities and differences between various Christian denominations and religious sects can usually be distinguished based on how one defines the above listed theological constructs. So too models of Christian counseling will differ based on how the meaning of these theological notions are employed by their respective authors.

Figure 6.1 below presents a diagram outlining these nine theological constructs.

Figure 6.1
Theological Dimensions of a Model of Christian Counseling

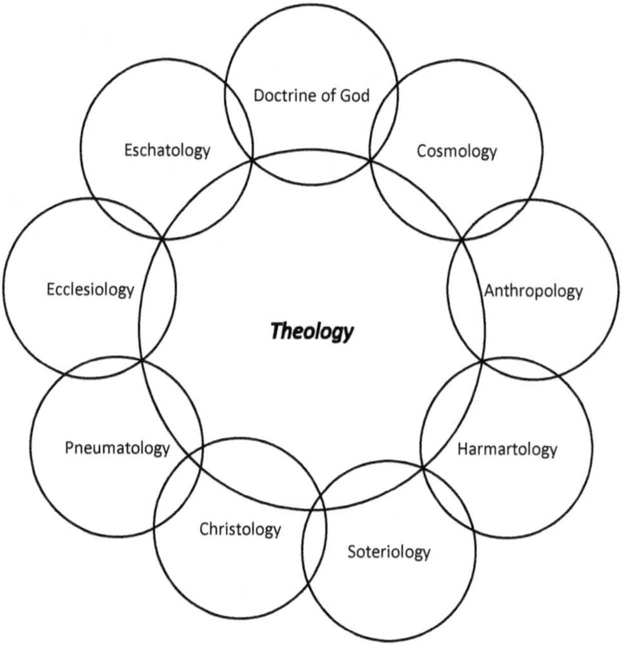

- Doctrine of God
- Eschatology
- Cosmology
- Ecclesiology
- Anthropology
- *Theology*
- Pneumatology
- Harmartology
- Christology
- Soteriology

PSYCHOLOGICAL UNDERPINNINGS

The process of exploring the *psychological underpinnings*[2] of a particular model of Christian counseling involves ascertaining to what extent the author incorporates elements of one or more of the following psychologies as outlined by Jones and Butman (1991).

---

2. For a review of various attempts to integrate certain psychological models with the practice of Christian counseling, see especially Shafranske (1996, 391–533) and the *Journal of Psychology and Theology* 25 (1997): 81–163. See also Jones and Butman (1991).

- Dynamic psychologies, including classical psychoanalysis, contemporary psychodynamic psychotherapies, and Jungian therapy.
- Behavioral psychologies, including behavioral therapy, rational-emotive therapy, and cognitive-behavioral therapy.
- Humanistic psychologies, including person-centered therapy, existential therapy, gestalt therapy, and transactional analysis.
- Family systems psychologies, including various forms of family therapy.

Models of Christian counseling will differ based on the psychological presuppositions that they embrace.

Figure 6.2 below displays the psychological underpinnings.

Figure 6.2
Psychological Dimensions of a Model of Christian Counseling

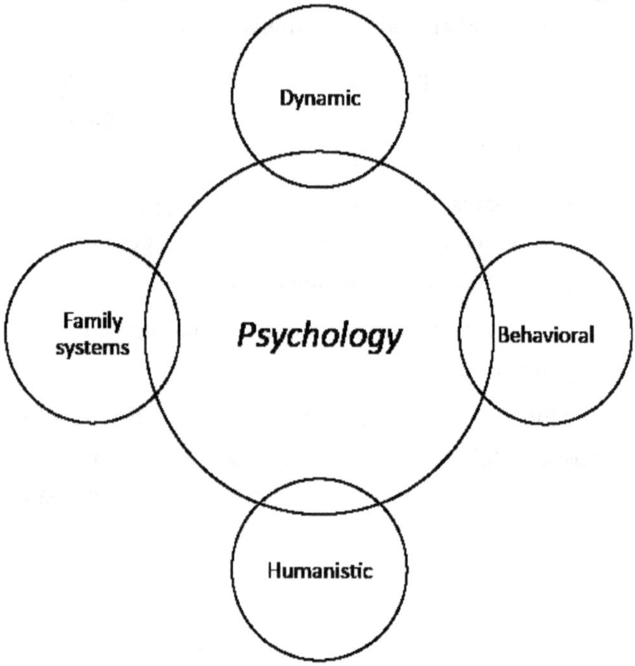

(Diagram: central circle labeled "Psychology" overlapping with four surrounding circles labeled "Dynamic" (top), "Family systems" (left), "Behavioral" (right), and "Humanistic" (bottom).)

SPIRITUAL UNDERPINNINGS

The process of exploring the spiritual underpinnings or the use of spiritual intelligence in a particular model of Christian counseling involves ascertaining the degree or extent that the author incorporates spiritual resources in the counseling process and or advocates the perfection of certain Christian virtues or character traits.[3] Spiritual resources might include but are not limited to:

3. For a review of how spiritual resources and or virtues have been incorporated into the practice of Christian counseling, see especially Miller (1999) and McMinn (1996).

- Surrender, confession, forgiveness
- Prayer, meditation, study and memorization of Scripture
- Baptism, communion, worship
- Solitude, fasting
- Restitution, service, witnessing

Virtues[4] might include but are not limited to:
- Gratitude, humility, integrity, serenity
- Faith, hope, love
- Joy, peace, patience, kindness, goodness, faithfulness
- Meekness, self-control, righteousness, endurance, godliness

Models of Christian counseling differ in their incorporation and usage of spiritual resources and the virtues or character traits they might emphasize.

Figure 6.3 below outlines spiritual resources and character traits:

---

4. Biblically, virtues are referred to as fruit of the spirit. See especially Galatians 5:22–23, 1 Timothy 6:11, and 2 Timothy 2:22.

Figure 6.3
Spiritual Dimensions of a Model of Christian Counseling

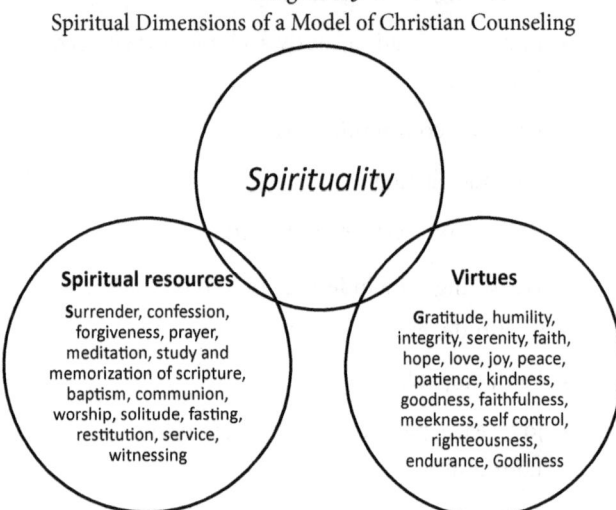

THEOLOGICAL, PSYCHOLOGICAL, AND SPIRITUAL

Figure 6.4 below summarizes the three factors in need of examination in order to adequately evaluate a model of Christian counseling. The figure suggests that there is an overlap between the three factors. Figure 6.5 below summarizes the three factors but suggests that there is no overlap.

Evaluating Models of Christian Counseling 77

Figure 6.4

Theological, Psychological, and Spiritual Dimensions of a Model of Christian Counseling

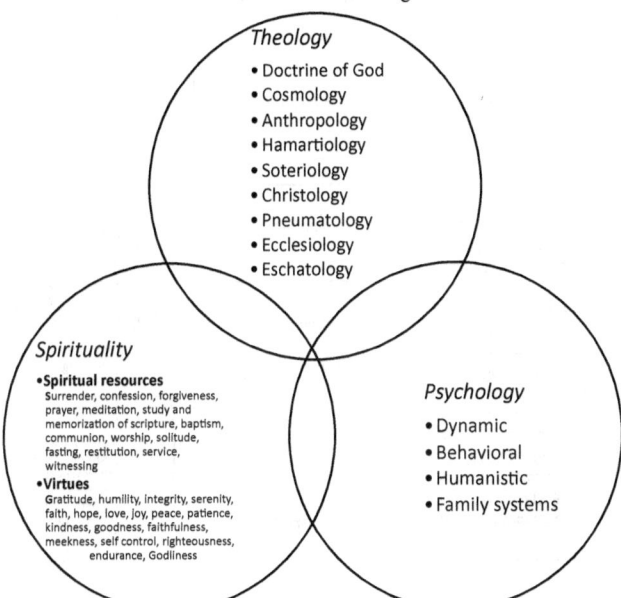

Four different models of Christian counseling have been selected to demonstrate how to effectively utilize the paradigm presented. Chapter 7 examines the "nouthetic" counseling model of Jay Adams. Evaluated in chapter 8 is Bill Gothard's "basic life principles" model of Christian counseling. Chapter 9 reviews Robert McGee's "search for significance" model of Christian counseling. Chapter 10 outlines Kenneth Haugk's model of "Christian caregiving."

Figure 6.5
Theological, Psychological, and Spiritual Dimensions of a Model of Christian Counseling

Theology
- Doctrine of God
- Cosmology
- Anthropology
- Hamartiology
- Soteriology
- Christology
- Pneumatology
- Ecclesiology
- Eschatology

Psychology
- Dynamic
- Behavioral
- Humanistic
- Family systems

Spirituality

Spiritual resources
Surrender, confession, forgiveness, prayer, meditation, study and memorization of scripture, baptism, communion, worship, solitude, fasting, restitution, service, witnessing

Virtues
Gratitude, humility, integrity, serenity, faith, hope, love, joy, peace, patience, kindness, goodness, faithfulness, meekness, self control, righteousness, endurance, Godliness

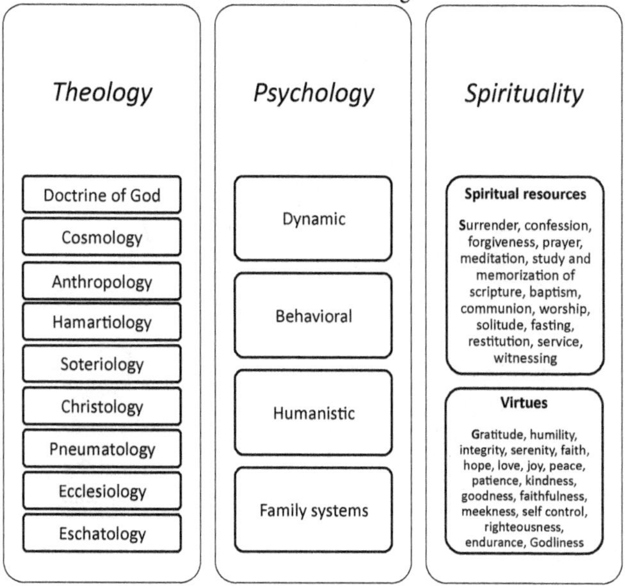

FUEL FOR THOUGHT

1. What other questions need to be addressed in evaluating a model of Christian counseling?
2. What does it mean to say a person has spiritual intelligence?
3. How does humanistic counseling differ from biblical counseling?
4. How does humanistic psychology differ from dynamic psychology?
5. How do you incorporate Christian virtues into the counseling process?

7

Jay Adams's Nouthetic Counseling

THEOLOGICAL UNDERPINNINGS

THE UNDERPINNINGS of Jay Adams's nouthetic model of Christian counseling are presented in three separate texts written over a ten-year span of time. These texts include his 1970 book, *Competent to Counsel*, his 1973 writing, *The Christian Counselor's Manual*, and his 1979 transcript, *More Than Redemption: A Theology of Christian Counseling*. Key to comprehending each of these texts is a thorough understanding of Adams's representation of the Greek term *nouthesis* and his notion of nouthetic confrontation.

Adams (1970, 44–64) explains that the Greek word *nouthesis* vacillates in translation "between the words 'admonish,' 'warn,' and 'teach'" and sometimes is translated as "counsel." One translator renders it "put sense into." Arguing that *nouthesis* has "no exact English equivalent," Adams suggests that the word is best understood as both "a concept and a practice." Nouthetic confrontation, therefore, consists of three basic elements.

One element of nouthetic confrontation involves a type of teaching that "presupposes the need for a change in the person confronted." The teaching, the making of information "known, clear, understandable, and memorable," may or may not be welcomed. Nonetheless, the person confronted has done something wrong and faces "some sin, some obstruction, some problem, some difficulty, and some need that has to be acknowledged and dealt with." Adams points out, therefore, that "the fundamental purpose of nouthetic confrontation is to effect personality and behavioral change."

The second element of nouthetic confrontation involves employing biblically legitimate "verbal means . . . the training by word of mouth . . . a person to person verbal communication" aimed at "straightening out the individual by changing patterns of behavior to conform to biblical standards." Emphasis is placed on the verbal exchange to get the receiver to focus on the "what" of their problem instead of the "why." Adams explains that the "why" is already known. We get into trouble in our "relationships to God and others" because of our sinful nature. This aspect of nouthetic confrontation, therefore, stresses "personal conference and discussion" for the purpose of bringing about "greater conformity to biblical principles and practices."

The third element of nouthetic confrontation "implies changing that in his life which hurts the counselee." Adams explains: "The goal must be to meet obstacles head on and overcome them verbally, not in order to punish but to help him." The motive for advising, admonishing, and warning the counselee of the error of his or her ways must be "love and deep concern, in which clients are counseled and corrected by verbal means for their good, ultimately, of course, that God may be glorified." Therefore, nouthetic confrontation is scriptural confrontation, using "the principles and practices of the Scriptures" to help the counselee develop a pure heart, a good conscience, and a sincere faith.

Adams is quite explicit about his understanding of God. His doctrine of God emphasizes that God is omniscient, omnipresent, and omnipotent. Adams (1979, vii) explains: "God must be omniscient to know all aspects of a situation in order to answer prayer... he must be omnipresent to hear all prayers uttered at all times and in all places ... he must be omnipotent in order to respond to every circumstance in any way that he wishes" and it takes a "God who is all three to bring about his universal goals through each particular in the universe in relation to every other particular both in the past and future as well as in the present."

Adams (1979, 47–84) points out that effective counseling requires the counselor to both believe in and express to the counselee the "sovereignty of a beneficent God," explaining "that things are that way because they are in God's plan and under God's control, and that through them he will work all such things for his good and the good of his people."

Adams's cosmology emphasizes that God is a living God who is the "person in charge." Adams explains that "God is in charge of the counselor, the counselee, and the counseling." God will not "strike bargains or compromise with the counselee ... abandon his wisdom to accommodate the foolishness of human wisdom ignorance ... stop loving to conform to the counselee's hatred and bitterness... forget his own holiness to overlook the counselee's unholy desires." Therefore it is "the counselee who must conform to his environment God, not the other way around."

Adams also emphasizes that God is a God of justice. Although many of our experiences may appear unjust, their imbalance is only temporary, for "the picture is larger than it may seem." Circumstances must be reviewed in light of the cross in a world "where a good God reigns." We learn from God's many names the revelation of "his provisions, his care, his protection, his concern, his faithfulness." For God is the source of all wisdom, help, correction, and blessing. Adams (1973, 35–36) emphasizes the biblical principle that "it is only the long-term that can fuse short-term purposes and goals into a meaningful overall pattern." God therefore is "the Alpha and Omega, and his Son, Jesus Christ, is the One who is the same yesterday, today, and forever." Thus "all purposes take on ultimate meaning only in relationship to him. Apart from him, they are simply isolated short-term objectives which randomly come and go without any necessary connection and, thus, no ultimate purpose."

In conclusion, Adams "reemphasizes the fact that God is man's basic environment. . . . God is around us, in us, and with us." But our rebelliousness resulted in our estrangement and alienation from God. In an unregenerate state, we remain uncertain, void of absolutes and standards outside of ourselves, never sure about our lives, antagonistic toward God, and ultimately "unhappy and uncomfortable with" our environment.

Adams's (1979, 118–61) theological anthropology stems from his systematic study of Scripture. He concludes that it is our "likeness to God" that makes us "different from the animals. That in part at least, though some say this is the whole of it, "we are intelligent, morally responsible creatures." We are, as was Adam, "material, spiritual, moral, and social beings." And because of Adam, we are also totally depraved—"corrupted in all areas of life, though not totally corrupt in each." We are "sinners perverted from birth" capable of developing "sinful response patterns" from the beginning of our lives that foster problems in all of life situations. Counselors, therefore, "must discover and help Christians find God's solutions to these human problems caused by sin."

Adams's harmartiology, or doctrine of sin, results from his systematic study of the Word as revealed in the Old and New Testament. Adams (1979, 147–52) explains that sin incorporates many meanings as indicated by such words as: "bent, breaking up or ruin, rebellion against a rightful authority, revolt, treason, not knowing which way to turn, tossing, a breach of trust, unfaithfulness, treachery, vanity, guilt through negligence or ignorance, fall short of, miss the mark, trouble, travail, weariness, unjust, unfair, crossing the boundary line, lawlessness, disobedience to a call, falling when one should stand upright, ignorance of what one ought to know, defect, shortcoming." These descriptions, Adams points out, speak of either the act, state of, or the effects of sin. For sin, Adams concludes, is "lawlessness, disobedience to God . . . failure to what God requires or any transgression of what he forbids." Sin involves more than alienation in human relationships, it involves "a personal affront to the Creator" that results in an alienation from God.

Adams's (1979, 177–248) soteriology, or his doctrine of salvation, embraces the Reformed tradition. Adams explains that salvation is the core reason why Christian counseling is possible: "It is the foundation or basis for all counseling." Noting the "impossibility of counseling unbelievers," proper counseling involves "working with saved persons to enable them to make changes at a level of depth that pleases God." Salvation equips the sinner with the Word and Spirit of God, creating a genuine hope "based on the unfailing promises of God that he has recorded in the Scriptures." It is the saved person who is privy to both God's direction and the power to achieve it. Dependency on human strength is replaced by the "written, revealed Word of God." "No matter what the problem is," Adams claims, "the far-more-abounding nature of the grace of Jesus Christ in redemption will make the difference in our counseling."

Adams emphasizes that the good news is that "Christ died for our sins a penal, substitutionary, sacrificial death and that he rose bodily from the dead (cf. 1 Cor. 15:3). This good news must be announced to all: proclaiming a new way of thinking that leads to faith and forgiveness and repentance (*metanoia*). Adams explains that repentance is literally "a change of mind; a rethinking. . . . Repentance refers to a change of heart—a new orientation of the inner man brought about by the Holy Spirit. It involves a rethinking of one's relationships toward God, one's self, sin, Christ, others. . . . It leads to the conclusion that 'I am a sinner who must trust Christ alone for forgiveness of sin.'" Repentance after repentance leads to a similar conclusion: "I have sinned against my heavenly Father; I must ask him to forgive me through Christ." Repentance is known to be genuine when the inner changes of heart lead to outer changes in life. The two are connected but must never be confused.

Salvation involves our reconciliation with God. It entails confession and forgiveness leading to the establishment of a new relationship with God. It involves a confession that acknowledges "on our part that we *agree* with God in what he has said about our sin in his Word. We stand on his side—the side of the One offended—and acknowledge that he is right in holding us guilty of an offense." This confession results in our acknowledgement of our "guilt and liability" to God and others we have wronged. It involves asking for forgiveness with the hope of "establishing of a new and better relationship, replacing enmity and alienation with peace and fellowship."

Adams's (1979, 174–82) *christology*, his study of the person and work of Jesus Christ, also stems from a Reformed view. He contends that without Christ's atoning sacrifice our reconciliation with God would not be possible, and the conduct of Christian counseling would be futile. Believing Christ to be the "incarnate Son," Adams asserts that Christ presented God's plan for human salvation. For Jesus's life, death, and resurrection "was a carefully thought through, well planned, and precisely executed program." Christ's death saved us from "the penalty of sin justification ... the power of sin sanctification ... and from the presence of sin glorification."

Carefully linked to his views of soteriology and Christology are Adams's (1979, 264) notions about pneumatology, the doctrine of the Holy Spirit. Whereas Christ's death makes reconciliation possible, his resurrection and ongoing presence in the form of the Holy Spirit makes change possible. We no longer need to linger in the aftermath of our shortcomings but we can embrace new, lasting, and sustaining virtues. Adams explains: "Because the Spirit works in the inner person, to change one's thinking and attitudes, counselors will focus on inculcating the biblical data that (1) set the standards for Christian behavior, and that (2) point to specific principles and practices of Christian living." Counselors will take the time "to show how practically these can be integrated into the particular situation that each counselee faces. Since the Holy Spirit uses the Scriptures, they can count on him in his own way and time to bless their faithful ministry of the Word."

Adams's ecclesiology (1979, 281–82), the study of the church as a biblical and theological topic, is underscored by his insistence that "every new convert should be encouraged to obey Jesus Christ immediately." He argues that "we should not wait until someone gets into trouble months or years later in order to instruct him." While emphasizing the need to teach converts basic doctrine and encouraging them to engage in regular "Bible study, prayer, church attendance, and witnessing," he points out that "the greatest need for a new convert," however, "is to recognize that his life *as a whole* must change. Christ wants him to be different across the board." Every congregation, therefore, "must have a purposeful plan and practical program to accomplish this."

Adams's (1979, 300–7) view of eschatology, the study of the end of the world, emphasizes that there will be "a judgment for all after death." Cautioning that we should not be "trying to take the sting out of death apart from the cross of Christ," we should remember that "a fearful anticipation of judgment and the fury of fire" belongs to "God's adversaries." Unfortunately for many, "existence in eternal separation from God" awaits them, forgoing "the blessings and joys of living with and serving God for eternity." For Adams notes that "the Bible teaches there will be a judgment for all after death."

Adams (1973, 4) emphasizes that God "holds each one of us personally responsible for his thoughts, words, and actions regardless of external pressures and influences." All will appear "before the judgment seat of Christ," each of us will "be recompensed for his deeds in the body, according to what he has done, whether good or bad." But, Adams (1973, 41) explains, there is "hope for the *eschaton*, the last time, the future." The coming of Christ, "the resurrection of the body and the erasure of sin, pain, and tears . . . with its crowning hope—the presence of Christ . . . the hope and expectation of final perfection"—all this gives us reason to have hope. But, Adams emphasizes, the abundant life is also available now. As we apply the gospel to the alleviation of our sinful behavior, the believer can experience and "enjoy the peace, comfort, and assurance of the fullness of the living Christ here in this life."

In summary, we can conclude that the theological underpinnings of Adams's nouthetic counseling stress to the reader that "truth and godliness are interrelated in such a way that it isn't possible to have one without the other, and that, therefore, counselors must become biblical theologians if they would see their counselees grow by God's grace."

PSYCHOLOGICAL UNDERPINNINGS

Adams (1979, xi–xii) makes it perfectly clear that "psychiatric and psychoanalytic dogmas" have no place in the church, for these beliefs are "every bit as pagan and heretical and therefore perilous as propagating the teachings of some of the most bizarre cults." In fact, Adams explains, "The cults are less dangerous because their errors are more identifiable, since they are controverted by existing creedal statements." Adams (1973, 9–10) further elaborates: "Biblically, there is no warrant for acknowledging the existence of a separate and distinct discipline called psychiatry. There are, in the Scriptures, only three specified sources of personal problems in living: demonic activity (principally possession), personal sin, and organic illness. These three are interrelated. All options are covered under these heads, leaving no room for a fourth: non-organic mental illness." Adams emphatically concludes that "there is, therefore, no place in a biblical scheme for the psychiatrist as a separate practitioner."

Adams (1973, 33–34) for example, takes exception to Christian writer Gary Collins, who advocates that "neither psychology nor theology has a clear statement about the nature of man." Adams argues that such statements that there is no "biblical view of man" reveal "a profound ignorance of the history and results of theology and exegesis." Besides, Adams contends, it is futile "to attempt to find reality in the eclectic fusion of Christian theology and psychological speculation." Additionally, Adams (1973, 92) points out, "The Bible does not need to be 'balanced' off by modern psychology. Nor may it be 'combined' with psychology to construct a balanced approach."

For Adams (1979, xiii), therefore, the Bible, not psychology, "is the basis for a Christian's counseling," for it "deals with the same issues that all counseling does." The Bible "was given to help men come to saving faith in Christ and then to transform believers into his image." Adams

(1973, 92) elaborates: "God sets forth *his* approach in the Scriptures. The principles of his approach are plainly revealed in his Word." Adams further adds that "on the basis of these principles, not in combination with Rogerian, Freudian, or Skinnerian principles, he may discover that some aspect of non-Christian methodology in some way may remind, illustrate, or amplify a biblical principle." Adams warns that "the principle must be scriptural. From a biblical foundation, upon which a house of biblical methodology has been constructed, a Christian counselor may view the surrounding landscape. But he must not construct his foundation or house out of any non-Christian materials."

Even though Adams strongly denunciates any association with psychological principles or their usage, review of his therapeutic model indicates a close resemblance to many of the principles and practices of the behavioral psychologies, especially cognitive-behavioral therapy. For example, in his defense of nouthetic counseling Adams (1979, 170) writes: "The charge that nouthetic counseling cares little about cognitive matters is absurd indeed; it is seriously misleading." Continuing his argument, Adams explains: "It is questionable whether any other system of counseling, purporting to be biblical, has (1) ever attempted to consider the various dimensions of such instruction as thoroughly, or (2) enjoined teaching so forcefully and insistently." Adams (1979, 166–67) explains how "human sinful thought has so perverted biblical values that an entire system of such value reversal could be developed and seriously entertained as an option by many." Self-actualized living "grounded on selfishness, desire for power, wealth, etc., rather than on the desire to live in a way that pleases God . . . this hedonism is directly opposed to the Christian emphasis to 'seek first' ... and to 'lose your life.'" Such convictions, he points out, have created "an intellectual-moral battle ... not merely the battle for the mind" but "a battle for the whole man." We must, therefore, with Paul "tear down arguments and every high barrier that is raised against the knowledge of God [in order to] take every thought captive and bring it into obedience to Christ."

Further evidence of a cognitive-behavioral approach to counseling is noted when Adams (1979, 168–69) writes about counselees adopting "erroneous explanations of life." He explains that in such instances the counselor must call the counselee "to repentance, a change of thinking, for his arrogance against God and for believing and living lies. Positively, they must present God's truth and call him to believe and walk according to it."

Similar examples are noted in Adams's (1979, 263–64) explanation of sanctification. He writes: "How, then, does sanctification take place? Patterns of thinking and living change as one is "renewed by the Spirit" who is working in his "mind" (Eph. 4:23).

While I have considered in part the human side of this renewal (vv. 22, 24), I must here say a word about the Spirit's work in renewing God's image by renewing the mind (cf. Col. 3:9–10; Rom. 12:1–2). Because the Spirit works in the inner person, to change one's thinking and attitudes, counselors will focus on inculcating the biblical data that (1) set the standards for Christian behavior, and that (2) point to specific principles and practices of Christian living.

Or, observe Adams's (1970, 68–69) explanation of repentance "as a change of mind leading to a new outlook in which faith in Christ brings about a change of purpose and a change of direction." Also note how Adams's (1973, 191) presentation of a seven-step change process parallels the thinking of many cognitive-behavioral therapists (for example, see Ross [1994, 77–82]).

1. Becoming aware of the practice (pattern) that must be dehabituated (put off);

2. Discovering the biblical alternative;

3. Structuring the whole situation for change;

4. Breaking links in the chain of sin;

5. Getting help from others;

6. Stressing the whole relationship to Christ;

7. Practicing the new pattern.

Indeed, the evidence strongly suggests that Adams's model of nouthetic counseling mirrors many of the precepts of cognitive-behavioral therapy, especially the notions of dysfunctional thoughts and the principles of change.

SPIRITUAL UNDERPINNINGS

Adams would advocate the usage of any and all spiritual resources that are clearly delineated in Scripture. As previously clarified, the Bible serves as the foundational basis for nouthetic confrontation. Adams (1979, xiii–xiv) explains: "The Bible is the basis for a Christian's counseling because of what counseling is all about: changing lives by changing values, beliefs, relationships, attitudes, behavior. What other source can provide a standard for such changes? What other source tells us how to make such changes in a way that pleases God?" Therefore, Adams concludes, "That is why other foundations for counseling must be rejected. Not only are they not needed—the Bible is adequate (the unique One, Who is the Counselor, proved that by his own counseling ministry)—but since they seek to do the same sorts of things without the Scriptures and the Spirit, they are also competitive. God doesn't bless his competition! Nor does he bless disobedience to his Word by his servants." Therefore, we as counselors are to be "ministers of the Word," being careful not to "forsake the fountain of living water for the cracked cisterns of modern counseling systems."

Second in primacy as a spiritual resource for Adams would be the usage of prayer. Adams explains that it is important to pray, "asking God for wisdom, help, correction, and blessing upon our undertakings" as counselors. Adams (1979, 62) explains: "The counselor must pray for himself and his counselees, asking God to use his Word as it is ministered in the counseling sessions, requesting wisdom for himself in the selection, understanding, and use of the Scriptures in gathering and analyzing data according to biblical norms, and seeking God's help in preparing the soil in the counselee's heart inner life for the sowing of the scriptural seed." Usage of prayer in this manner reinforces our understanding of the basic biblical principle "that all that is happening is taking place in the presence of God, for his glory and in dependence on him."

Adams (1979, 61–76) also concludes that prayer is an essential part of the confession and salvation processes and is also important in both the commitment phase and the thanksgiving phase of counseling. But Adams cautions that prayer should not "stand alone as the biblical solution to a problem." To the complaining counselee who remarks that "I prayed about it and nothing happened," we should emphatically respond with the rhetorical question, "Did you pray that the Lord would give you the strength and wisdom to *do*?" Therefore, for Adams, prayer has a "central place in Christian counseling, both for the counselor and for the counselee." Consequentially, any counseling that fails to incorporate prayer, "the power of God that transforms counselees," is essentially non-Christian. Subsequently, prayer "must have a prominent place, since both counselor and counselee must ask for God's help and depend upon him to give it."

The biblical notions of acceptance, surrender, confession, and forgiveness, especially as understood within a context of salvation, are also useful spiritual resources in Adams's (1979, 172–217) model of nouthetic counseling. For counseling to be successful, the counselee must not entertain any illusions and must come to full acceptance of the "realities of human sin and error." The counselee must surrender to the facts, that dependence or our "own sinful wits or the counselor's for change" is insufficient, for it is the Word and the Spirit that "provide all that is necessary to renew the mind (Rom. 12:1–2) and enable us to understand, believe and obey."

Surrender leads to confession. Not a catharsis per se, but essentially an agreement, "an acknowledgment on our part that we agree with God in what he has said about our sin in his Word. We stand on his side—the side of the One offended—and acknowledge that he is right in holding us guilty of an offense." Confession becomes a formal acknowledgment of the fact that "I have sinned; I am liable

... it involves a personal, on-the-record admission of guilt." Confession leads "quite naturally to asking forgiveness from God and those others who may have been wronged, followed by the granting of forgiveness and the establishing of a new and better relationship to them." Adams explains: "A forgiving person, then, is one who is no longer held liable for his sin. He cannot be held accountable (cf. Rom. 3:19). Clearly, according to this usage, something is held against someone until he is forgiven. But when forgiveness occurs, he is freed from that condition; nothing is held against him anymore. That liability to, or threat of punishment has been lifted, removed; it has been let go and has gone away."

Adams emphasizes that "forgiveness never ignores sin or tolerates it, accepting the other person as he is; rather, forgiveness is forgiveness of sin seen to be, acknowledged, and repented of as sin." Forgiveness, he explains, "focuses on the fact that there was an offense; it does not turn away from this fact but deals with it." He also warns that "psychological doctrines of acceptance are cheap substitutes for forgiveness" because they "deny the need for and efficacy of Christ's atonement," nor do they make demands for changing the sinful behavior. For psychological notions of change ignore the importance of a sense of guilt, the need to confess it, and the importance of forgiveness. For it is in our acceptance, surrender, and confession that God is able to forgive us and thus restore our relationship to him.

The development of Christlike virtues, or what is commonly referred to in the Bible as "fruit of the spirit," is at the heart of Adams's (1979, 249–62) model of nouthetic counseling. Adams contends that the "goal of sanctification is not only to put off the works of the flesh, but in its place to put on the fruit of the Spirit. He elaborates: "Growth is gradual; man can assist producing it, but cannot initiate it or assure its production. Fruit cannot be manufactured, but growth may be promoted by providing such important elements as light, water, nutrients, etc. The growth of fruit depends upon care and cultivation. Counselors ministering the Word work under the Spirit in his orchard to provide such care. So, then, both the progressive nature of sanctification and the necessity for care and cultivation are aptly depicted by the term "fruit."

He further explains: The production of the Spirit's fruit, then, involves human agency; it is not procured passively, but by "pursuing" it. The pursuit of fruit is a large factor in the task of Christian counseling. We must discover how this pursuit of fruit takes place in counseling and how the Spirit produces fruit in the life of its pursuers. A discussion of these factors must precede a consideration of the individual items that are designated "fruit."

Adams concludes that the "pursuit of fruit in counseling is a top priority." They "become goals for Christian counselors to pursue in all their counseling." Therefore, it is essential that the Christian counselor "understand the basic meaning of each term and how it may be pursued." Counselors must become "adept at locating such lacks in their counselees, identifying strengths and weaknesses, and in describing each quality in depth." In short, "they must understand the Spirit's fruit thoroughly." Emphasizing that the Bible claims that our personality is fluid rather than certain, that is, susceptible to the changing influence of God and the Holy Spirit, Adams explains that nouthetic confrontation can help counselees effect personality change.

This is accomplished by encouraging counselees to pursue the "fruit of the spirit." Adams explains:

> The Spirit's fruit, from one perspective, may be said to consist of a fairly comprehensive list of desirable personality traits, the acquisition and development of which ought to be a goal of counseling. It is safe to say that a person who has learned to produce such luscious fruit in profusion is a person who has overcome his difficulties and except for occasional instructive guidance, perhaps needs no further counseling. So, the pursuit of fruit in counseling represents the positive or, to use the language of Paul elsewhere, the "put on" side of sanctification.

Therefore, fruit of the spirit will emerge when we teach our counselees how to pray, regularly study the Bible, and daily apply the principles of Scripture to our lives.

FUEL FOR THOUGHT

1. What does Adams mean by the words *nouthetic counseling*?
2. What are the key theological elements emphasized in Adams's model for Christian counseling?
3. What is the difference between CBT counseling and biblical counseling?
4. What importance does Adams place on using prayer and Scripture in his model for counseling?
5. Do you have to be a confessing Christian in order to benefit from biblical counseling?

8

Bill Gothard's Basic Life Principles

THEOLOGICAL UNDERPINNINGS

CENTRAL TO comprehending Bill Gothard's (1981, 5) model of Christian counseling is grasping his notion of seven "basic life principles." He explains: "Underlying all the basic teachings of Christ there are significant principles which are essential for successful living." These principles include design, responsibility, authority, suffering, ownership, freedom, and success. The principle of *design* encompasses God's "precise purposes for each person" from which we derive "our identity and fulfillment on life." *Responsibility* emphasizes that "God holds us personally responsible for every one of our words, thoughts, actions, attitudes, and motives." *Authority* reminds us that "God has established a structure of authority and a balance of power," a system of accountability. *Suffering* embraces ordained grace "for personal cleansing, growth, and achievement by learning how to properly respond to those who offend us." *Ownership* enables us "to conquer anger and worry as we acknowledge that all we have is from him and belongs to him." *Freedom* directs us to God's power to do his will in "morals and finances," enabling us "to serve others in love." *Success* helps us to rejoice in the knowledge that "God conquered the world, the flesh, and the devil through the death, burial, and resurrection of Christ." By engrafting these scriptural truths "into our soul," a renewed mind emerges equipped with God's power to "live above the law of sin." But when one or more of these basic principles of God are "violated or neglected," Gothard cautions, "breakdowns result in one or more of these basic relationships of life: response to God, acceptance of self, family harmony, purpose for the future, effectiveness in friendships, harmony in dating and marriage, management of financial affairs."

Gothard explains that the root cause of our problems resides in our resistance to God's grace. Our stubbornness and/or open rebelliousness produces a dependence on our natural inclinations which subsequently lead to the violation of one or more of God's seven basic principles. These violations produce characteristics of "bitterness, greed, and moral impurity." These in turn foster attitudes of "inferiority, frustration, anger, envy, jealousy, insecurity, discontent, guilt/fear, lust/passions, and pride." These attitudes fuel visible actions of "wrong dress, slander, profanity, lying/flattery, stealing, vandalism, drugs/rock music, pornography, and arguments."

Counseling for Gothard (1993, 4–8), therefore, consists of helping the counselee identify the basic principle (or principles) being violated and then assisting the counselee in taking "clear and logical steps of action" necessary "to reconstruct thinking and direction." Critical to this process is introducing the counselee to the appropriate Scripture that serves as the foundation for the seven "basic life principles" and that "strengthen and reaffirm" the steps taken to correct the violations. For a counselor's responsibility, Gothard insists, is "to assist people in tracing surface problems to root causes," helping the counselee "to distinguish between his natural inclinations and the non-optional principles of God's Word," going beyond one's "own perspective" to "see a problem or circumstances from God's point of view." It is a counselor's responsibility to explain "biblical disciplines which promise to reward" and to urge "believers to accept them as a part of their lives." This process involves "helping a person resolve fear, depression, anger, lust, and other destructive emotions by relating them to 'strongholds' which can be torn down with biblical truth."

The goal for therapy, therefore, becomes one of helping the client achieve self-acceptance by building spiritual maturity. Gothard (1987, 4–5) points out that this spiritual maturity, learning God's design for your life, is achieved through the development of a good conscience by proper submission, obtaining full forgiveness, yielding of our rights, actively pursuing moral purity, and by meditation. Applying the principle of responsibility produces a good conscience. The success principle is achieved through meditation and the engrafting of Scripture into the soul. Authority occurs when we properly submit to God and his designated authorities. Freedom happens when we pursue moral purity. Suffering, in light of God's grace for righteousness' sake, yields full forgiveness. Ownership results in our yielding rights to God. Applied collectively, these six principles illuminate the principle of design as we experience an increased understanding of our identity and how to find genuine fulfillment in life. Therefore, the application of these six principles reveals God's "precise purposes for each person, object, and relationship."

Examination of Gothard's writings, especially his twelve-part series on principles of counseling (Gothard 1993–99), divulges a fairly precise depiction of his doctrine of God and his notions about cosmology. Gothard's theology begins by stressing the exclusiveness of God—"thou shalt have no other gods before me (Exodus 20:3)." God's nature is revealed, Gothard (1998, 5) explains, "by the names he has given himself. . . . He is the God who provides . . . who heals . . . leads to victory over the flesh . . . cleanses us and sets us apart for his work . . . the God who gives us peace . . . the God who is our righteousness . . . our shepherd . . . the God who is always present."

Subsequently, the ultimate life purpose "for everything God created is to glorify him." Gothard (1998, 20) explains: "The chief purpose of mankind is to know God and to glorify him forever. . . . The goals of the believer should be to help as many as possible become rightly related to God through his Son, the Lord Jesus Christ, and to grow in Godly character." It is this life purpose and commitment to this life goal that shapes our life calling and our life work. Our life serves, then, as a "written account . . . a life message . . . a treasure for future generations." For God is the source of all creation. He created us in his image so that we could have fellowship with him. God, explains Gothard (1995, 4), is "three Persons in One." He formed us "out of the dust of the ground (body), and breathed into our nostrils the breath of life (spirit), and we became a living soul (soul)."

Quoting 1 Thessalonians 5:23, that our "whole spirit and soul and body be preserved blameless," Gothard points out that our relationship to God is understood in the context of these three aspects of our being.

Gothard's (1998, 2–32; 1993, 2–12; 1993, 6–8) theological anthropology and his notions of harmartiology, soteriology, Christology, and pneumatology are best understood in relationship to his thinking about the spirit, soul, and body of a person and the condition of a person's heart. Gothard explains that the control center of human life and spiritual activity commences with the condition of a person's heart (*kardia*). Our spirit (*pneuma*), "the home of conscience, faith, genuine love, wisdom, discernment, drive, creativity, joy, and enthusiasm," is directed by and influenced by the condition of the heart.[1] A clean heart is one that is modeled after God's unblemished heart, as humanly demonstrated by the incarnate Christ. Our problems begin, however, when our spirit and eventually our soul (*psuke*)—that is, our mind, will, and emotions—become directed by an unclean or sinful heart. Gothard elaborates: "The sin nature that Adam passed on to all of us has corrupted and defiled every heart that is conceived except the heart of Jesus, because he was conceived by the Holy Spirit." Therefore, "the heart is deceitful above all things, and desperately wicked . . . from birth, our natural desires are opposite to the will and ways of God. . . . In this condition

---

1. Gothard (1998, 3–32) identifies twelve conditions of the heart that separate our spirit from God's spirit. They include a wicked heart, double heart, foolish heart, hard heart, bitter heart, proud heart, deceitful heart, lean heart, unbelieving heart, whorish heart, deceived heart, and discouraged heart.

we are under the wrath of God . . . God is angry with the wicked every day." But a clean heart is possible, Gothard emphasizes, not by "the result of our own efforts" but by "the work of God." For it is through "the sacrificial death of the Lord Jesus Christ God cleanses our heart of sin. . . . 'The blood of Jesus Christ his Son cleanseth us from all sin' (1 John 1:7)." For an unblemished, spotless, blameless heart is only possible through the blood of Jesus Christ. Gothard stresses that whereas the blood of Christ cleanses the heart, the Word (*logos*) of God cleanses the soul. Embracing God's grace in Christ enables God to restore the spirit. Engrafting his Word into our souls replaces the "pseudo-religious and pseudo-intellectual" mindsets that have been so instrumental in separating us from true fellowship with God.

Gothard contends that critical to our salvation is how we confront guilt and address these strongholds, these "mindsets and conclusions contrary to Scripture," that lead to the violations of God's seven basic principles. Initially fostered by "natural curiosity, the awakening of conscience, sensual focus, and the questioning of God's Word," our inclination to violate God's principles results in outward sin and a "violation of the conscience." Too often, however, the sin and the ensuing feelings of guilt that accompany it are not dealt with immediate repentance (change) but with incomplete repentance—"sorrow over the consequence of sin but not over the sin itself." Gone uncorrected, this unresolved sin produces a double-mindedness (concupiscence). Gothard explains: "On one hand, the soul wants to be spiritual, but on the other hand, the soul wants to be sensual." Left to fester, double-mindedness eventually leads to the resolution of guilt by "compensation in religious activity—

making up for sin by performing religious or humanitarian service . . . or by self-inflicted hardships." The ensuing conflict, however, continues to persist in the soul. Ultimately, this profound inconsistency in beliefs can only be resolved by either embracing true repentance, that is, the confession of the sin and the changing of one's way by embracing the truths of Scripture, or by continuing to justify the sinful activity by "redefining morality" and ultimately reinterpreting Scripture "to fit with the immorality."

The latter course of action, Gothard (1981, 114–16) points out, unfortunately results in reprobation. This condition of strong delusions deteriorates the spiritual system to the point "that it is not able to or does not wish to comprehend a heaven or hell or God." Energized by a "corrupt mind," the reprobate is apt to claim "that under grace we are free to do what we want." Trapped by an enslaved soul, the reprobate "despises submission . . . speaks evil of those in authority . . . scoffs at spiritual truths which are beyond human reasoning . . . complains about moral strictness . . . develops new and fashionable philosophies . . . argues irrationally over pseudo-philosophies that contradict God's Word." Religion, therefore, for the reprobate, becomes a guise "to cover pride, lust, and rebellion."

Gothard (1981, 123) explains that integral to helping the reprobate change is teaching him or her to "walk in God's spirit." This walk commences when the reprobate receives Jesus Christ as his or her personal savior—"his spirit indwells in our life," Gothard elaborates. Filling his or her spirit with the Spirit of God impacts "the inward parts of the soul," transforming it "into the 'image of Christ.'" As the "Holy Spirit reveals thoughts, words, actions, or attitudes which need changing," a testing—"God's spirit versus our spirit"—surfaces. Yielding to the Holy Spirit becomes essential, for if the human spirit prevails, "God's spirit is grieved and his effectiveness ... is quenched." Resisting temptation is possible, however, by reinforcing the Holy Spirit's direction with "precise scriptural principles." Spiritual maturity will result "to the degree that we cooperate with the Holy Spirit in resisting Satan with the Word of God."

Ecclesiology for Gothard (1981, 140–53) encompasses helping parishioners take "basic steps toward becoming a whole person." The church must first proclaim God's good news of how "to be born again," opening our spirit to the Spirit of God by confessing "Jesus as my Lord," asking him "to come into my life and cleanse me of all my sin." Next the church must show the parishioner how "to transform the soul." Gothard explains: "Once we have been born again by the Spirit of God, we will continue to experience conflicting struggles in our mind, will, and emotions. But now the Spirit and the Word of God make it possible to 'be transformed by the renewing of our minds' (Rom. 12:2)." Gothard points out that the church must help individuals "determine areas of personal character deficiency and find large sections of Scripture relating to them." We then are able to "rebuild thought structures" by memorizing "God's thought structures ... saturating our minds with Scripture ... picturing each word and personalizing it to our circumstances," asking God "to show us how to turn that word into action which will build Christian character and lead others to salvation." Gothard makes clear that this process of transformation will refocus our emotions and redirect our goals, moving us from cold and lukewarm Christians to Christians on fire for God. We will learn how to "express irritations, disappointments, and heartaches through Scripture," readily accepting that "God will allow certain situations in our lives to expose us to a wide spectrum of emotion" enabling us to "gain a wider sensitivity and insight into the nature of God and the feelings of others." The church exists for the purpose of restoring the conditions of our heart to one that pleases God and of refurbishing of the soul by equipping it with God's Word; therefore when we become restored and equipped, we can become "more like his Son, the Lord Jesus Christ," and are thus better prepared to help those around us experience God's love.

A review of Gothard's writings reveals no direct reference to a specific view of the end times, that is, a clearly defined eschatology. But his writings, especially his notions of reprobation and the principle of success, suggest that there are specific consequences both in this life and after death for being estranged from the Spirit of God. Gothard (1990, 8) makes it clear, for example, that the reprobate "is one whose conscience is defiled. He believes wrong is right and that right is wrong. He speaks of freedom, yet he himself is the slave of his own degenerate nature. His mind is void of God's truth and wisdom, yet he supposes himself to be wise as he pursues death." But Gothard (1990, 3) also explains in his principle of success that "God conquered the world, the flesh and the devil through the death, burial, and resurrection of Christ." Therefore, hope is even available for the reprobate, for freedom from sin can be obtained "by understanding and fully obeying the truth of Scripture."

PSYCHOLOGICAL UNDERPINNINGS

In contrast to Jay Adams, Gothard makes no direct reference to psychology other than to caution that our counsel should help others avoid the psychological delusions of pseudo-intellectual philosophies and pseudo-religions that stem from human spirits or conditions of the heart not in tune with God's Spirit. He also points out that the Greek word for "soul" (*psuche*), from which the word *psychology* is derived, in Scripture refers to the mind, will, and emotions of a person. Careful examination of Gothard's writings do uncover a strong resemblance to behavioral psychologies, especially cognitive-behavioral therapy.

Evidence that Gothard is most akin to cognitive-behavioral psychology is best illustrated in his notions of "strongholds" and the prescriptions he offers to conquer sinful habits. As defined previously, strongholds consist of well-rehearsed "mindsets contrary to Scripture." Effective counseling, Gothard (1993, 10–12) contends, requires the "pulling down of strongholds" by "identifying wrong ideas ... clarifying wrong actions ... pointing out wrong emotions." Effective counseling involves "explaining God's commandments ... learning from God's biographies ... revealing God's ways." Effective counseling leads others to "wise decisions," helping them to establish "daily disciplines," preparing them to give "appropriate testimonies ... transforming problems into life messages." Change occurs, Gothard (1990, 10–15) explains, when we "engraft Scripture into our souls ... meditate on it day and night ... picture ourselves dead to the power and appeal to sin ... make no provisions for sinful habits ... experience Christ's victory over sin ... are accountable to God-given authorities for victory... yielding self as an instrument of righteousness to God."

SPIRITUAL UNDERPINNINGS

Similar to Jay Adams, Gothard will utilize any and all spiritual resources that are consistent with Scripture. Most utilized by Gothard, however, is the study of, memorization, and meditation on Scripture. Gothard (1981, 144) explains: "If we are to think God's thoughts after him, we must be able to comprehend and appreciate his structure of thinking as presented in Scripture. The best way to do this is to memorize whole thoughts and ideas from Scripture.... Saturate your mind with Scripture.... Saturate your minds with God's Word.... It will wash out thoughts opposed to Scripture and will reconstruct other ideas around God's principles." Gothard concludes that it is through Scripture that we are able to rebuild thought structures that will be consistent with God's truth.

Gothard (1981, 124–28) also outlines in his writings the benefits of fasting. He contends that the practice of fasting will "increase spiritual alertness." He explains: "Our ability to perceive God's direction in life is directly related to our ability to sense the inner promptings of his Spirit. God provides a specific activity to assist us in doing this." Elaborating, Gothard asserts how the suspension of eating and exercise increases the amount of blood available "for mental and spiritual concentration." Fasting therefore should be "combined with Scripture memorization and meditation" with a "focus on reaching specific spiritual objectives." For example, we might want to use fasting to focus on "detecting temptation, conquering moral impurity, discerning God's will, identifying genuine love, and increasing spiritual growth." The Christian leader too would be encouraged to fast twenty-four hours prior to an important decision or the deliverance of an important message. Gothard concludes by explaining that fasting can be used for many purposes, including "spiritual alertness to overcome temptation, to seek God's will in a specific matter . . . repentance for sin . . . concern for the work of God . . . deliverance or protection . . . to humble oneself before God . . . as a part of worship . . . when in deep sorrow." For the purpose of fasting is to realize a "greater effectiveness in discerning and achieving God's purposes."

Gothard (1981, 171–72) insists that one of the most important purposes of a friendship is "to assist one another in developing Christlike character qualities." For to do so is in accord with what Gothard (1981, 151) describes as "God's ultimate purpose." We are to "become more and more like his Son, the Lord Jesus Christ" and to "reproduce his life in the lives of those around us." For God's purpose for us is spiritual maturity. This involves the development of virtues or character qualities. Gothard explains that spiritual maturity "means building the principles of God's Word into a person's life so that he is equipped to understand and follow the promptings of the Holy Spirit in knowing how to respond to any situation with Christlike attitudes." And to this end, Gothard identifies forty-nine character qualities amplified by Scripture, with love (as defined in 1 Corinthians 13) being most prominent.

FUEL FOR THOUGHT

1. What does Gothard consider to be "basic life principles"?
2. How would you summarize Gothard's view of salvation?
3. Is Gothard's theology consistent with his psychology?
4. What are the limitations of Gothard's model?
5. Upon what underlying assumptions does Gothard's model rely?

9

Robert McGee's Search for Significance

THEOLOGICAL UNDERPINNINGS

FOUR THEOLOGICAL terms form the core of McGee's (1998, 28–29) model of Christian counseling. They include *justification, reconciliation, propitiation*, and *regeneration*. McGee explains that justification "means that God has not only forgiven me of my sins but has also granted me the righteousness of Christ." Cloaked in Christ's righteousness, "I am therefore fully pleasing to the Father." Reconciliation "means that although I was one time hostile toward God and alienated from him, I am now forgiven and have been brought into an intimate relationship with him." For this reason, "I am totally accepted by God." Propitiation "means that by his death on the cross Christ satisfied God's wrath." Consequently, "I am deeply loved by God." Regeneration "means that I am a new creation in Christ." Armed with this knowledge of Scripture, the counselor can assist the counselee in either avoiding, or if necessary, helping the counselee climb out of, the mind traps of performance, approval, blame, and shame. Because our search for significance is rooted in justification, reconciliation, propitiation, and regeneration, McGee explains, people in Christ no longer "must meet certain standards to feel good . . . be approved by certain others to feel good," think of themselves as "unworthy of love" and deserving "to be punished," nor erroneously conclude that they "cannot change" or continue to harbor thoughts of hopelessness.

McGee's (1994, 1998) writings imply a doctrine of God and cosmology that places God as the source of and at the center of all creation. Citing Psalm 139 as his source, McGee (1994, 45–49) claims that God knows us thoroughly, protects us, is always present, is a sovereign Creator, has a plan for us, and is constant and consistent. His writings also indicate a theological anthropology that purports a humanity that initially was in full fellowship with God. McGee (1998, 13–14) explains: "The first created man lived in unclouded, intimate fellowship with God. He was secure and free. In all of God's creation, no creature compared to him. Indeed, Adam was a magnificent creation, complete and perfect in the image of God, designed to reign over all the earth (Gen. 1:26–28). Adam's purpose was to reflect the glory of God." McGee emphasizes: "Through man, God wanted to demonstrate his holiness (Ps. 99:3–5); love and patience (1 Cor. 13:4); forgiveness (Heb. 10:17); faithfulness (Ps. 89:1, 2, 5, 8); and grace (Ps. 111:4). Through his intellect, free will, and emotions, man was to be the showcase for God's glorious character." But as McGee's harmartiology would express, humanity's rebelliousness tarnished our fellowship with God, and thereby incurred his wrath. Fortunately, however, McGee's (1998, 15–18) soteriology and high Christology give hope for the removal of this garnishment from our souls. He elaborates: "Though we justly deserve the wrath of God because of that deliberate rebellion, his Son became our substitute, and he experienced the wrath our rebellion deserves." Further explaining: "Because Christ paid the penalty for our sins, our relationship with God has been restored, and we are able to partake of his nature and character, to commune with him, and to reflect his love to the entire world." Therefore we are freed to "Spread the good news! Man is not lost forever! God has not given up on us! He has bought us out of slavery to sin with the payment of Christ's death on the cross. Satan's rule can be broken, and we can reign with Christ." We can now rejoice because we have been "restored to the security and significance for which we have been created—not simply in eternity but here and now as well."

McGee stresses, therefore, that "we must never forget that God wants his children to bear his image and to rule with him ... we can still have the privilege of fellowship with him." McGee explains that "God has provided the solution." The question that still remains, however, is, "Will we accept Christ's death as the payment for our sins and discover the powerful implications of our salvation, or will we continue to follow Satan's lies and deceptions?" Are we willing to "give up our own efforts to achieve righteousness" and instead "believe that Christ's death and resurrection alone are sufficient to pay for our sin and separation from God?"

McGee emphasizes that saying yes to Christ by placing your trust in him generates "many wonderful things," including: "all your sins are forgiven: past, present, and future (Col. 2:13–14); you become a child of God (John 1:12; Rom.

8:15); you receive eternal life (John 5:24), you are delivered from Satan's domain and transferred into the kingdom of Christ (Col. 1:13); Christ comes to dwell within you (Col. 1:27; Rev. 3:20); you become a new creation (2 Cor. 5:17); you are declared righteous by God (2 Cor. 5:21); you enter into a love relationship with God (1 John 4:9–11); you are accepted by God (Col. 1:19–22)." But unfortunately, McGee concludes, far too many reject God's truth and "choose instead to believe Satan's lie." They continue "to reject God's truth and offer of salvation through Jesus Christ," choosing in its place to put their trust in "success and the opinions of others" to provide a sense of self-worth.

McGee's (1998, 53, 128–30) pneumatology emphasizes that the Holy Spirit is our source for change. The Holy Spirit "gives us encouragement, wisdom, and strength as we grow in our desire to honor the Lord." Regeneration, Mcgee explains, "is the renewing work of the Holy Spirit that literally makes each believer a new person at the moment trust is placed in Christ as Savior." McGee further clarifies that the Holy Spirit, "the third person of the Trinity, is God and possesses all the attributes of deity." The Holy Spirit helps us focus on and glorify Christ as "he guides us into the truth of the Scriptures." The Holy Spirit enables us, by his power, to experience the "love of Christ" flowing through us, "producing spiritual fruit within us." It is the power of the Holy Spirit that makes possible our "intimate friendship with Christ." It is the power of the Holy Spirit that produces "love for one another (John 15:12); joy and peace in the midst of difficulties (John 14:27; 15:11); steadfastness (Eph. 5:18–21); and evangelism and discipleship (Matt. 28:18–20)."

Review of McGee's writings does not reveal a specific ecclesiology or a definitive eschatology. But one can surmise from his writings that the cornerstone of his view of church would emphasize the significance of justification, reconciliation, propitiation, and regeneration as an ongoing message to be continually echoed. Failing to do so, he would argue, will relinquish the parishioner to the lies of Satan, causing one to linger in a present hell fueled by the mind traps of performance, approval, blame, and shame. McGee (1998, 129–30) explains: "Just as the cross of Christ is the basis of our relationship with God, it is also the foundation of our spiritual growth. Christ's death is the supreme demonstration of God's love, power, and wisdom. The more we understand and apply the truths of justification, propitiation, reconciliation, and regeneration, the more our lives will reflect his character." McGee adds that "spiritual growth is not magic. It comes as we apply the love and forgiveness of Christ in our daily circumstances. It comes as we reflect on the unconditional acceptance of Christ and his awesome power and choose to respond to situations and people in light of his sovereign purpose and kindness toward us."

McGee (1998, 121) concludes it is in these "four great doctrines" that we learn to experience "the stable and secure identity we have in Christ . . . experience his love, forgiveness, and power; and to express our appreciation of him to others." He further emphasizes that "because of justification, you are completely forgiven and fully pleasing to God. You no longer have to fear failure. Because of reconciliation, you are totally accepted by God. You no longer have to fear rejection. Because of propitiation, you are deeply loved by God. You no longer have to fear punishment, nor do you have to punish others. Because of regeneration, you have been made brand new, complete in Christ. You no longer need to experience the pain of shame." For it is with these "four great doctrines" that we undo and defeat the false beliefs perpetuated by Satan.

PSYCHOLOGICAL UNDERPINNINGS

The reviewed writings of McGee make no specific reference to psychology per se, but McGee's notion of regeneration and his outline for change is very similar in content to behavioral psychologies, especially, cognitive-behavioral therapy.[1] For example, McGee (1998, 149–50) writes: "For you to correct your thought process is hopeless unless you cooperate with God to release his power in your mind." Change, he explains, requires us to ask God to "renew our mind." Therefore his approach, like cognitive-behavioral therapy, emphasizes the importance of self-talk. But McGee explains that "renewing of the mind" involves more than self-talk. It is "more than repeating some words over and over. It is actually changing some of the thought patterns by which we have lived our entire lives." If true change is to occur we must, McGee argues, agree with God that "we have been deceived . . . we have been believing a lie and we need to repent for doing so." We must allow God "to show us how destructive this lie has been in our lives." We must choose "to reject the lie we have been believing so long and committing ourselves to believe what God says to be true." We

---

1. Note especially how McGee's four primary false beliefs parallel the irrational notions as presented by Ellis and other cognitive-behavioral therapists. For example, see Ross (1994, 80).

must be "willing to stand on the truth that God discloses to us about ourselves instead of using our normal responses."

SPIRITUAL UNDERPINNINGS

The underlying goal of McGee's approach to Christian counseling is to bring about a spiritual change in the life of the counselee. McGee (1994, 192–221) recommends the usage of several spiritual resources, especially surrender, confession, forgiveness, prayer, meditation, Scripture, restitution, service, and witnessing, as a means to achieve this purpose. Surrender, confession, and forgiveness, McGee (1994, 10–11) explains, entails a five-step process that includes admitting our powerlessness over sin and the unmanageability of life that it creates; coming to believe and trust in Christ as a means to alleviate and correct our sinful lifestyle; choosing to repent by deciding to turn our will and life over to God through Christ; taking inventory of our past wrongs; and experiencing freedom through confession by admitting to God, ourselves, and another person the exact nature of our sins. Coalesced, these five steps restore our relationship with God.

Continued growth in our relationship with God is accomplished through prayer, meditation, and Scripture. For example, in discussing prayer, McGee explains that "effective prayer" incorporates praise, petition, thanksgiving, and confession. Praising God helps to develop humility—"recognizing that we are people of infinite worth because God loves us, but we are not God." Petitioning God reminds us that we need to ask him for help instead of relying on our own volition. God wants to embrace "the concerns and burdens of your heart." Expressing thanksgiving—"showing gratitude for what God does for you," this "attitude of gratitude" is a "wonderful replacement for bitterness and pride." Confessing our sins to God in prayer encourages us to take inventory of ourselves and enables us to "experience forgiveness and renewed fellowship with God."

McGee also encourages the incorporation of meditation into our daily routine. Meditation—"spending time thinking about, contemplating, or pondering the things of God"—will produce "a clearer understanding of and deeper relationship with God." In contrast to Eastern religions that encourage "emptying the mind of conscious thought," McGee explains that Christian meditation encourages the filling of the mind with Scripture. McGee elaborates:

> You will find the greatest value in meditating on Scripture. If possible, memorize the Scripture passage so you can recall it and reflect on it at any time. Focus your thoughts on certain parts of the passage as you create a mental picture. Reflect using all of your senses—seeing, hearing, tasting, smelling, and touching—as you do the activity. Ask questions about the passage, formulate answers to related problems or needs, and commit to apply or use what you have learned.

McGee concludes that Christian meditation "is both a mental and spiritual process of thinking, conversing, planning, anticipating, and reflecting." Meditation is a means of "developing and enriching one's spiritual devotion."

McGee emphasizes that learning God's Word and then obeying it is also essential for our spiritual growth. For it is by our study of Scripture that we learn the "attributes of

God . . . God's commands . . . God's promises . . . God's warnings." We must first learn God's truths if we expect to begin applying his truths in our lives. When combined with prayer, meditation, and Bible study, these truths, McGee argues, will greatly enhance our relationship with God.

Spiritual growth is also enhanced by forgiving those who have wronged us and in making restitution or amends to those we have harmed or offended. Forgiveness of others necessitates "giving up our self-proclaimed right to blame, condemn, find fault, punish, and retaliate against others." Restitution involves asking those we have harmed or offended to forgive us and, when possible, restoring to the person that which we lost or took away. Service and witnessing encompasses reaching out to others in need of God's healing love and grace, being willing to testify to how God has transformed your life. McGee explains: "An ambassador represents his or her country. In the same way, you represent the kingdom of God and the One who called you into the freedom you now experience. You have the privilege of sharing with others how they can become free. Helping others is, in part, the telling of a story. The story tells about our progress toward health through the power of Jesus Christ. . . . Everyone needs the message that Jesus Christ is the answer to the sin problem."

Character development, or the obtainment of Christian virtues, is also an integral ingredient of McGee's model of counseling. Character defects, for the most part, are rooted in the erroneous mindsets that generate a "fear of failure . . . of rejection . . . of punishment and the compulsion to punish others," and underlying unresolved shame about oneself. Unfortunately, if gone uncorrected, these

Satanic mindsets will destroy, or at a minimum block the development of, Christian virtues. Instead they will foster "perfectionism, avoiding risks, anger, resentment, pride, depression, low motivation, sexual dysfunction, chemical dependency, addiction to success, identity entangled with success, sense of hopelessness, anger at ourselves and God... being easily manipulated, codependency, avoiding people, negative messages, hypersensitivity to the opinions of others, hyposensitivity... self-induced punishment, bitterness, passivity, punishing others, fears of all sorts . . . inferiority, habitually destructive behavior, self-pity, isolation and withdrawal, loss of creativity, despising our appearance." However, McGee emphasizes that this despair is avoidable if we are only willing to incorporate into our thinking the good news offered by justification, reconciliation, propitiation, and regeneration.

FUEL FOR THOUGHT

1. What is the significance of justification in McGee's model for counseling?
2. What is the significance of reconciliation in McGee's model for counseling?
3. What is the significance of propitiation in McGee's model for counseling?
4. What is the significance of regeneration in McGee's model for counseling?
5. What does McGee mean when he entitles his writings "search for significance"?

10

Kenneth Haugk's Christian Caregiving

HEOLOGICAL UNDERPINNINGS

A CORE assumption underlying Haugk's (1984, 19–21) "caregiving" model of Christian counseling centers on his assertion that God is the ultimate "cure giver," whereas we are simply the caregivers. He explains: "The apostle Paul knew this. In 1 Corinthians 3:6–7 he writes, 'I planted, Apollos watered, but God gave the growth. So neither he who plants nor he who waters is anything, but only God who gives the growth.'" As a farmer's responsibility rests with preparing a crop for harvest, so the Christian caregiver's responsibility is to "plant" and "water." God then provides the growth. In other words, "Christians are responsible for care; God is responsible for cure." Haugk points out that when a caregiver realizes "that God is the cure giver," it eliminates "worry and false expectations." Focus then shifts from getting results to concentrating on "creating the best therapeutic situation for growth to occur: developing trust and communicating acceptance and love."

Underlying Haugk's core assumption is a doctrine of God and a cosmology that asserts the universe was created by a caring God to whom we can call upon in times of trouble and rejoice with in good times. Haugk (2000, 66–76) uses various Scripture references to portray a God who "cares about us in our grief . . . has overcome death, shares our grief with us . . . knows what it is like to have a loved one die." He presents a God "who is with us and comforts us . . . knows the pain and fear of death . . . stays with us in our dying." He describes a God "who is always with us . . . who cares for us when we are ill . . . cares about our needs and can provide for them . . . a God who gives us peace, wisdom . . . and still loves us after all we have done." He depicts a God of "mercy and forgiveness" who "values us highly," a God who knows rejection and betrayal and understands anger. He puts forth the picture of a God that people "need and long for," a God who can deliver us from our human condition.

Unfortunately, not all of humanity currently experiences a caring relationship with a loving God. Haugk (1984, 50–51) explains: "Created by God, people necessarily live their lives in relationship to God. Relationships with God vary significantly among individuals and across time. Some individuals are angry with God and alienated from him, at least part of the time. Others have a relationship that can most kindly be characterized as cool or distant. Still others experience a close relationship with God—finding meaning, purpose, value, and dignity in that relationship." Yet even these people, bonded to God like a child to a parent, find themselves gripped by questions that go to the very heart of their existence: "What is the meaning of life? Why am I here? How does God view me? What is right, and what is wrong? Why does God allow suffering? Why must I die?" These key questions cut to the center of a person's "genuine spiritual needs." They cannot be ignored, Haugk contends, for "they are part of the flow of human life."

Haugk's (1984, 65) harmartiology acknowledges that sin produces a "brokenness and separation from God." This "fragmentation destroys families, friendships, and individuals." Sin erects a wall that alienates us "from others and seals off hope for reconciliation." Haugk's soteriology and Christology,[1] however, present a message of hope. He explains: "Into the shattered remains of God's perfect creation comes the message that Jesus Christ brings the gift of wholeness to anyone able to accept it. It is the gift of salvation won by Christ's death and resurrection and received through faith that has torn down the separating wall of sin and restored our relationship with God. The Greek word for "to save" (*sodzo*) also means "to heal" and "to make whole." It is a gift of life offering to make people whole forever, beginning right now. It is this salvation, this healing, that takes broken, shattered lives and re-creates them infinitely "better than new."

Haugk readily admits that "human beings constantly fall short of God's expectations. All have faults, failings, and imperfections that repeatedly cause us to fall before God and say with the prodigal son, 'Father, I have sinned against heaven and before you; I am no longer worthy to be

---

1. Haugk's (1984, 118) Christology especially portrays Jesus as the incarnate son of God. He explains: "The Bible relates how God sent his Son Jesus to become a human being so that he could bring love, healing, hope, forgiveness, and new life to the world."

called your son' (Luke 15:21)." But he offers encouragement when he reminds us that "one of the richest resources of the Christian faith is the surprising gift of forgiveness that God offers us through Jesus Christ. God freely offers forgiveness to everyone. Christians throughout the ages have found special comfort and renewed life in the promise of forgiveness."

Haugk explains that "God shares this message of forgiveness through his people." His ecclesiology, therefore, stresses the need for the church to be a place where people can experience God's forgiveness and God's love. "As members of the body of Christ," he writes, "Christians have Jesus's command to extend God's gracious offer of forgiveness to one another (John 20:23)." For it is through the church and its membership that the care and love of God is conveyed to others. And it is through specially trained lay people[2] within the congregation that the care and love of God can be greatly enhanced and be readily dispersed to people in need of it.

But Haugk's (1984, 35) pneumatology stresses "the message of God's love grips Christians" as "we are filled by the Holy Spirit." The Holy Spirit "moves clay-footed Christians to use our God-given gifts for others. He makes cared-for Christians into caring Christians."

Review of Haugk's writings indicates no particular viewpoint with regards to eschatology. While acknowledging the inevitability of death and the theological and spiritual

---

2. Haugk calls these specially trained lay persons Stephen ministers. They undergo fifty hours of training designed to produce skilled, trustworthy, compassionate caregivers who can convey to people in need, through the sharing of their faith in Christ, the care and love of God.

questions that it presents, Haugk's writings present no definitive position on the study of last things, the end of the world, or the nature of life after death.

PSYCHOLOGICAL UNDERPINNINGS

Haugk (1984, 45–49) is quick to point out how his "caregiving counseling" is unique and significantly differs from psychological approaches to counseling. He explains:

> Disciples of Sigmund Freud often claim that the only real, non-superficial way to diagnose and treat the individual is to employ psychoanalytic perspectives and techniques, that is, investigating the unconscious, focusing on childhood, dream analysis, and free association. "We know where the action is," they seem to say. "It's infantile sexuality, libido, the Oedipus complex, and ego defense mechanisms. If you are unwilling to tackle the problem at those depths, you're just playing around."

Further commenting, he writes:

> While the Freudian system does have value, and in many ways is indeed a deep system, when compared to the uniquely Christian system of caring for the individual, it is quite superficial. Infantile sexuality and libido do not seem so deep next to the basic questions and concerns of life, death, spirituality, and meaning. These latter issues reach down to the deepest level of our beings—beyond the unconscious. . . . The same applies to a number of psychological systems: Rogerian, behavioral, gestalt, rational-emotive,

transactional analysis, and neo-analytic, to name a few. I believe each of these systems has a unique and valuable contribution to make. Nevertheless, these approaches appear quite superficial when compared to the unique Christian perspective.

Haugk reminds his readers that Christian caregiving differs from psychological approaches because it can touch spiritual depths that psychology cannot. He emphasizes that it has only been in the last fifty to seventy-five years that "emphasis has shifted from a theological to a psychological basis for Christian caring and counseling." Christians, he argues, "need to recover something that they once possessed, but recently lost: theology as the primary source out of which caring and counseling flows." Haugk concludes: "Psychology, sociology, and medicine cannot give the entire answer to the human condition. There is a significant gap left for theology, and it behooves Christians, both clergy and lay, not to disavow their authority, but to step in and fill that gap."

Haugk (2000, 677) contends that we must fill this gap with "gospel-centered caring" that helps people develop a "loving, trusting relationship with God." Gospel-centered caring, Haugk explains, recognizes that "God alone builds this relationship," especially "through the presence, prayers, witness, and care of Christian caregivers." Recognizing first "what Jesus has done for the care-receiver and what the Holy Spirit continues to do," the "gospel-centered caregiver" also acknowledges what God has done for them. Motivated then "by a sense of gratitude," they are able to communicate God's grace, inviting "others to experience God's incredible goodness in Jesus." Armed with a willingness to share their own vulnerability and their need for God's grace, these gospel-centered caregivers are able to convey to others "how God's love gives strength, hope, and courage to people in whatever circumstances they face."

Although Haugk is insistent that his "Christian caregiving model" differs significantly from psychological approaches to counseling, a careful review of his notions reveals a marked similarity to humanistic psychologies, especially client-centered therapy as presented by Carl Rogers. This is especially evident when he introduces such notions as empathy and genuineness as means to building the counseling relationship, and when he stresses the importance of active listening as a primary source to accomplishing counseling goals.[3]

SPIRITUAL UNDERPINNINGS

Providing "spiritual care" is one of the cornerstones of Haugk's (2000, 659–95) model of counseling. For it is important as Christians that we help people "hear and believe that God loves them." Haugk explains: "People . . . need special care for spiritual pain, understand better the reasons for those spiritual needs, and know even how to give and receive spiritual care." Growth in faith also occurs as we understand better our needs "for spiritual care and the resources you can turn to for help." These spiritual resources may include reading biblical stories, recalling biblical

---

3. In fairness to Haugk, it is important to emphasize that his model is designed to be implemented by laypeople. Therefore, usage of a non-directive approach that stresses active listening may best serve his purpose and help avoid ethical and legal entanglements that might emerge in using other more directive approaches.

promises, prayer, meditation, fasting, journaling, worship, participating in the sacraments, confession, forgiveness, absolution, and fellowship with other Christians.

These spiritual growth enhancers, these "conduits of grace," help people to become "aware of God's presence." They help reduce worry by increasing faith, recognizing and believing that "God is caring for us." They generate hope as we learn to be more positive knowing that "God is in charge." They improve our ability to love as we learn to "care for those in need." They generate an attitude of gratitude as our growing knowledge of God's love for us helps us to be more open to God's grace. Repentance and humility emerge as we are now able "to freely admit our faults and turn away from our sins when we become aware of them." Christian community becomes important. "We love and serve others," sharing "what God has given," learning to seek guidance from fellow Christians. These spiritual outcomes show evidence of God's grace working in our lives.

Christian character traits of gratitude and humility emerge as we demonstrate to others God's love in our sharing of our faith and hope in Christ. Armed with the power of God through Christ, we can help others confront the circumstances of "ignorance, oppression, suffering, shame, despair, and evil" that prevent them and us from fully experiencing God's love. Our example serves to help the nonbelievers who are brazen out their choice of "refusing to believe," assisting them in facing their "anger with God" or their "unwillingness to forgive." Our encouragement in Christ motivates them to meet head-on their idolatrous thoughts and sinful desires that produce the pride and guilt that distract them from truly appreciating God's love, or discourage them from fully participating in a Christian community of faith. As we demonstrate to others our spiritual growth by sharing how God's grace and the indwelling power of the Holy Spirit has changed our lives, our Christian witness assists others in overcoming their "choices and circumstances" that have circumvented their encounter with a loving God, and have deprived them form experiencing the sweet fruit that stems from abiding in Christ.

FUEL FOR THOUGHT

1. Compare and contrast Haugk's model of counseling with Adams's, Gothard's and McGee's.

2. What does Haugk mean when he states that caregiving is a way of life?

3. What precautions does Haugk need to consider when introducing a lay counseling program?

4. Identify the underlying assumptions in Haugk's model.

5. How does your view of God compare with Haugk's view?

Epilogue

IN THE previous ten chapters a framework for evaluating models of Christian counseling has been introduced within the context of the counseling process. The challenges inherent in incorporating psychological, theological, and spiritual principles into a model of Christian counseling have also been discussed. Four illustrations were also presented showing how to evaluate the effectiveness of a Christian counseling program in employing psychological, theological, and spiritual constructs.

This inquiry has revealed that each of the four writers has expounded a theological anthropology that clearly depicts a humanity separated from, alienated, and estranged from God, our Creator. Each author has presented a theological solution to humanity's predicament that minimally embraces the importance of allowing the love of God demonstrated in Christ to enter our lives. Each essayist has emphasized the importance of Scripture and prayer as essential spiritual tools for spiritual growth. Each has either directly or indirectly alluded to the importance of challenging unbiblical notions or mindsets contrary to Scripture as an important ingredient to fostering spiritual growth and to producing a permanent change in the condition of our hearts. Each has shown how their respective model of Christian counseling moves beyond the precepts of psychology. Each has skillfully argued that it requires the embrace of theological notions to tackle the ultimate issues of life and death. Each has seriously questioned the appropriateness of psychology's attempt to address such issues. Each has proposed that our ultimate concern should center on sharing with others, through our words and deeds, the love of God in Christ that dwells within us and the fruit of the Spirit that such love so bountifully produces.

Appendix

EVALUATING MODELS OF CHRISTIAN COUNSELING

Course Syllabus

CLASS MEETING TIME

Class will meet from 1:00p.m. to 4:00p.m. on Wednesdays.

COURSE DESCRIPTION

This three-hour course is especially designed to help students in the MA in Counseling program and/or the MDiv program to develop skills that will enable them to effectively evaluate models of Christian counseling. Students completing the course will develop sensitivity to the underlying psychological, theological, and spiritual dimensions of four specific models of Christian counseling, thereby learning how to compare and contrast the strengths and limitations of each model. Students will also learn how to evaluate the efficacy and efficiency of each approach as a legitimate means of counseling.

REQUIRED READINGS

———. 1970. *Competent to Counsel*. Nutley, NJ: P&R.

Bridger, F., and D. Atkinson. 1998. *Counseling in Context: Developing a Theological Framework*. London: Darton, Longman, and Todd.

Emmons, R. A. 1999. *The Psychology of Ultimate Concerns*. New York: Guilford.

Gothard, B. 1996. *A Comprehensive Course in Effective Counseling, Part 9: How the "Heart" Determines Direction in Life*. Oak Brook, IL: Institute in Basic Life Principles.

———. 1997. *A Comprehensive Course in Effective Counseling, Part 8: Anger Resolution*. Oak Brook, IL: Institute in Basic Life Principles.

———. 1998. *A Comprehensive Course in Effective Counseling, Part 11: Seven Basic Needs of Today's Youth*. Oak Brook, IL: Institute in Basic Life Principles.

Haugk, K. C. 1984. *Christian Caregiving: A Way of Life*. Minneapolis: Augsburg.

McGee, R. 1998. *The Search for Significance*. Nashville: Word.

Shafranske, E. P. 1997. *Religion and the Clinical Practice of Psychology*. Washington, DC: American Psychological Association.

COLLATERAL READINGS

Browning, D. S. 1987. *Religious Thought and the Modern Psychologies: A Critical Conversation in the Psychology of Culture*. 3rd ed. Philadelphia: Fortress.

Crabb, L. 1988. *Inside Out*. Colorado Springs: NavPress.

Jones, S. L., and R. E. Butman. 1991. *Modern Psychotherapies: A Comprehensive Christian Appraisal*. Downers Grove, IL: InterVarsity.

MacArthur, J. F. Jr. 1994. *Introduction to Biblical Counseling: A Basic Guide to the Principles and Practices of Counseling*. Dallas, TX: Word.

McMinn, M. R. 1996. *Psychology, Theology, and Spirituality*. Wheaton, IL: Tyndale.

Miller, W. R. 1999. Integrating Spirituality into Treatment. Washington, DC: American Psychological Association.

Van Deusen Hunsinger, D. 1995. Theology and Pastoral Counseling: A New Interdisciplinary Approach. Grand Rapids: Eerdmans.

COURSE OBJECTIVES

Upon completion of this course, students will be able to: *identify* the psychological, theological, and spiritual components of a model of Christian counseling; *compare and contrast* the psychological, theological, and spiritual assumptions underlying a model of Christian counseling; and *determine* the efficacy and efficiency of a model of Christian counseling within the context of the counseling process. In addition each student will gain an *appreciation* for and a better *understanding* of the complexity involved in attempting to integrate psychology with theology and spirituality.

COURSE OUTLINE

Class 1: The Counseling Process

Class 2: Psychology and the Counseling Process

Class 3: Theology and Spirituality and the Counseling Process

Class 4: Compatibility of Psychology with Theology and Spirituality

Class 5: Jay Adam's "Nouthetic Counseling"

Class 6: Jay Adam's "Nouthetic Counseling"

Class 7: Bill Gothard's "Basic Life Principles

Class 8: Bill Gothard's "Basic Life Principles"

Class 9: Robert McGee's "Search for Significance"

Class 10: Robert McGee's "Search for Significance"

Class 11: Kenneth Haugk's "Caregiving"

Class 12: Kenneth Haugk's "Caregiving"

Class 13: Comparison and Contrast of the Four Models

Class 14: Final Examination

Bibliography

Adams, J. E. 1970. *Competent to Counsel*. Nutley, NJ: P&R.

———. 1973. *The Christian Counselor's Manual: The Sequel and Companion Volume to* Competent to Counsel. Phillipsburg, NJ: P&R.

———. 1974. *The Christian Counselor's Casebook*. Grand Rapids: Baker.

———. 1975. *The Use of Scriptures in Counseling*. Phillipsburg, NJ: P&R.

———. 1977. *Lectures on Counseling*. Grand Rapids: Baker.

———. 1977. *The Christian Counselor's New Testament: A Translation in Everyday English with Notations, Marginal References, and Supplemental Helps*. Grand Rapids: Baker.

———. 1979. *More Than Redemption: A Theology of Christian Counseling*. Grand Rapids: Baker.

———. 1979. *Update on Christian Counseling*. Phillipsburg, NJ: P&R.

———. 1986. *The Biblical View of Self-esteem, Self-love, Self-image*. Eugene, OR: Harvest House.

Allen, C. L. 1953. *God's Psychiatry: Healing for the Troubled Heart and Spirit*. Grand Rapids: Revell.

American Association of Christian Counselors. 2000. *Caring for People God's Way: Certificate Program in Biblical Counseling*. Forest, VA: Center for Biblical Counseling.

American Psychological Association Online. 1999. www.apa.org. Washington, DC.

American Psychological Association Online. 2001. www.apa.org. Washington, DC.

Anonymous. 1984. *The Billy Graham Christian Worker's Handbook: A Layman's Guide for Soul Winning and Personal Counseling.* Minneapolis: World Wide.

———. 1996. *Reporting Child Abuse, Neglect, and Dependency.* Frankfort, KY: Kentucky Department for Social Services.

———. 1998. *AACC Christian Counseling Code of Ethics.* Forest, VA: American Association of Christian Counseling.

Arthur, G. L., and C. D. Swanson. 1993. *Confidentiality and Privileged Communication.* Alexandria, VA: American Counseling Association.

Arthur, K. 1988. *Lord, Heal My Hurts.* Portland, OR: Multnomah.

Balsbaugh, M., T. Gardner, B. Klabunde, W. Luce, B. Peil, S. Shores, and L. Sittig. 1998. *Counseling Insights: A Biblical Perspective on Caring for People.* 2 vols. Anaheim, CA: Insight for Living.

Bandler, R., and J. Grinder. 1975. *The Structure of Magic: A Book about Language and Therapy.* Palo Alto, CA: Science and Behavior Books.

Brammer, L. M. 1973. *The Helping Relationship: Process and Skills.* Englewood Cliffs, NJ: Prentice-Hall.

Bayles, M. D. 1981. *Professional Ethics.* Belmont, CA: Wadsworth.

Bennett, B. E., et al. 1990. *Professional Liability and Risk Management.* Washington, DC: American Psychological Association.

Bobgan, M., and D. Bobgan. 1979. *The Psychological Way/The Spiritual Way.* Minneapolis: Bethany.

Bond, T. 1993. *Standards and Ethics for Counseling in Action.* London: Sage.

Bridger, F., and D. Atkinson. 1998. *Counseling in Context: Developing a Theological Framework.* London: Darton, Longman, and Todd.

Brokaw, B. F. 1997. "Applying Theory in Clinical Practice: Clinical Integration of Psychology and Theology." *Journal of Psychology and Theology* 251: 81–85.

Browning, D. S. 1987. *Religious Thought and the Modern Psychologies: A Critical Conversation in the Psychology of Culture.* 3rd ed. Philadelphia: Fortress.

Bufford, R. K. 1997. "Consecrated Counseling: Reflections on the Distinctives of Christian Counseling." *Journal of Psychology and Theology* 251: 111–22.

Canter, M. B., B. E. Bennett, S. E. Jones, and T. F. Nagy. 1994. *Ethics for Psychologists: A Commentary on the APA Ethics Code*. Washington, DC: American Psychological Association.

Carter, J., and S. B. Narramore. 1979. *The Integration of Psychology and Theology*. Grand Rapids: Zondervan.

Chapman, G., and D. Chapman. 1997. *Five Signs of a Functional Family*. Chicago: Northfield.

Clouse, B. 1997. "'Can Two Walk Together, Except They Be Agreed?': Psychology and Theology—A Journey Together or Paths Apart?" *Journal of Psychology and Theology* 251: 38-48.

Collins, G. A. 1988a. *Christian Counseling: A Comprehensive Guide*. Rev. ed. Dallas: Word.

———. 1988b. *Can You Trust Psychology?* Downers Grove, IL: InterVarsity.

Colson, C. 1985. *Who Speaks for God? Confronting the World with Real Christianity*. Westchester, IL: Crossway.

Colson, C., and N. Pearcey. 1999. *How Now Shall We Live?* Wheaton, IL: Tyndale.

Comiskey, A. 1988. *Pursuing Sexual Wholeness: How Jesus Heals the Homosexual*. Santa Monica, CA: Desert Stream Ministries.

Crabb, L. 1988. *Inside Out*. Colorado Springs: NavPress.

———. 1991. *Men and Women: Enjoying the Difference*. Grand Rapids: Zondervan.

DeGroot, A. T. 1965. *Disciple Thought: A History*. Fort Worth, TX: Texas Christian University Press.

Dieter, M. E., A. A. Hoekema, S. M. Horton, J. R. McQuilkin, and J. F. Walvoord. 1987. *Five Views on Sanctification*. Grand Rapids: Zondervan.

Dobson, J. 1980. *Emotions: Can You Trust Them?* Ventura, CA: Regal.

Dyer, W. W., and J. Vriend. 1975. *Counseling Techniques That Work: Applications to Individual and Group Counseling*. Washington, DC: American Personnel and Guidance Association.

Dunnam, M. 1994. *This Is Christianity*. Nashville: Thomas Nelson.

Eisenberg, S., and D. J. Delaney. 1977. *The Counseling Process*. 2nd ed. Chicago: Rand McNally.

Emmons, R. A. 1999. *The Psychology of Ultimate Concerns*. New York: Guilford.

Farnsworth, K. E. 1985. *Wholehearted Integration: Harmonizing Psychology and Christianity through Word and Deed.* Grand Rapids: Baker.

Farnsworth, K. E., and M. W. Regier. 1997. *A Vision for the Future: Redeeming Psychology and Business, Managing Managed Care, and Partnering with the Church.* Journal of Psychology and Theology 251: 155–63.

Gardner, T., W. Luce, B. Peil, S. Shores, and L. Sittig. 1997. *Counseling Insights: A Biblical Perspective on Caring for People.* 2 vols. Anaheim, CA: Insight for Living.

Gleitman, H. 1995. *Psychology.* 4th ed. New York: W. W. Norton.

Gothard, B. 1981. *Research in Principles of Life.* Oak Brook, IL: Institute in Basic Life Principles.

———. 1982. *Rebuilder's Guide.* Oak Brook, IL: Institute in Basic Life Principles.

———. 1984. *Reviewing and Reaffirming Seventeen Basic Commitments: How to Protect Your Sons and Daughters by Cleansing Your Home.* Oak Brook, IL: Institute in Basic Youth Conflicts.

———. 1987. *How to Discover Purpose in Life: Applying Basic Principles.* Oak Brook, IL: Institute in Basic Life Principles.

———. 1992. *How to Tear Down the Strongholds of Bitterness.* Oak Brook, IL: Institute in Basic Life Principles.

———. 1993–1999. *A Comprehensive Course in Effective Counseling.* 12 parts. Oak Brook, IL: Institute in Basic Life Principles.

Grinder, J., and R. Bandler. 1976. *The Structure of Magic.* 2 vols. Palo Alto, CA: Science and Behavior Books.

Hall, M. E. L., and T. W. Hall. 1997. "Integration in the Therapy Room: An Overview of the Literature." *Journal of Psychology and Theology* 251: 86–101.

Hartley, John. 1981. *Salvation: An Inquiry into Soteriology from a Biblical Theological Perspective.* Anderson, IN: Warner.

Haugk, K. C. 1984. *Christian Caregiving: A Way of Life.* Minneapolis: Augsburg.

———. 2000. *Stephen Ministry Training Manual.* 2 vols. St. Louis: Stephen Ministries.

Hays, R. B., S. L. Jones, V. P. Furnish, et al. 1994. *Homosexuality in the Church: Both Sides of the Debate*. Louisville: Westminster John Knox.

Hemfelt, R., F. Minirth, and P. Meier. 1989. *Love Is a Choice: A Groundbreaking Book on Recovery for Codependent Relationships*. Nashville: Thomas Nelson.

———. 1991. *Love Is a Choice Workbook: Recovery for Codependent Relationships*. Nashville: Thomas Nelson.

Ivey, A. E., and L. Simek-Downing. 1980. *Counseling and Psychotherapy: Skills, Theories, and Practice*. Englewood Cliffs, NJ: Prentice-Hall.

Johnson, E. L. 1997. "Christ, the Lord of Psychology." *Journal of Psychology and Theology* 251: 11–27.

Jones, S. L., and R. E. Butman. 1991. *Modern Psychotherapies: A Comprehensive Christian Appraisal*. Downers Grove, IL: InterVarsity.

Jones, S. L. 1996. "A Constructive Relationship for Religion with the Science and Profession of Psychology: Perhaps the Boldest Model Yet." In *Religion and the Clinical Practice of Psychology*, edited by E. P. Shafranske, 113–48. Washington, DC: American Psychological Association.

Kelsey, M. 1986. *Christianity as Psychology*. Minneapolis: Augsburg.

Kirwan, W. 1984. *Biblical Concepts for Christian Counseling: A Case for Integrating Psychology and Theology*. Grand Rapids: Baker.

Koestline, K. H. 1970. *What Jesus Said about It: All the Words of Jesus Arranged according to Subjects*. New York: New American Library.

Koteskey, R. L. 1980. *Psychology from a Christian Perspective*. Nashville: Abingdon.

Kurtz, E., and K. Ketcham. 1992. *The Spirituality of Imperfection: Storytelling and the Journey to Wholeness*. New York: Bantam.

Kurtz, E. 1999. "The Historical Context." In *Integrating Spirituality into Treatment*, edited by W. R. Miller, 19–46. Washington, DC: American Psychological Association.

Ladd, G. E. 1996. *A Theology of the New Testament*. Rev. ed. Grand Rapids: Eerdmans.

Lake, F. 1966. *Clinical Theology*. London: Darton, Longman, and Todd.

Lakoff, G., and M. Johnson. 1980. *Metaphors We Live By*. Chicago, IL: University of Chicago Press.

Larson, B. 1987. *God Does Care*. Houston: J. Countryman.

Lewis, E. 1952. *Theology and Evangelism: Far-reaching Truth about God, Christ, and Man*. Nashville: Tidings.

MacArthur, J. F., Jr. 1991. *Our Sufficiency in Christ*. Dallas: Word.

———. 1993. *Anxiety Attacked: Applying Scripture to the Cares of the Soul*. Wheaton, IL: Victor.

———. 1994. *Introduction to Biblical Counseling: A Basic Guide to the Principles and Practices of Counseling*. Dallas: Word.

———. 1998. *Forgiveness: The Freedom and Power of Forgiveness*. Wheaton, IL: Crossway.

———. 1998. *The Pillars of Christian Character: The Basic Essentials of a Living Faith*. Wheaton, IL: Crossway.

Macon, M. D. 1997. *Theology: The Doctrines of the Christian Faith*. http://home.wmis.net/~ixthys/thlgy.htm

Martin, J. E., and C. R. Carlson. 1988. "Spiritual Dimensions of Health Psychology." In *Behavior Therapy and Religion: Integrating Spiritual and Behavioral Approaches to Change*, edited by W. R. Miller and J. E. Martin, 57–110. Newbury Park, CA: Sage.

McGee, R. S., and W. D. Mountcastle. 1993. *Conquering Eating Disorders: A Christ-Centered 12-Step Process*. Nashville: LifeWay.

McGee, R. S., D. W. McCleskey, P. Springle, and S. Joiner. 1994. *Conquering Chemical Dependency: A Christ-Centered 12-Step Process*. Nashville: LifeWay.

McGee, R. 1998. *The Search for Significance*. Nashville: Word.

McKim, D. K. 1996. *Westminster Dictionary of Theological Terms*. Louisville: Westminster John Knox.

McMinn, M. R. 1996. *Psychology, Theology, and Spirituality*. Wheaton, IL: Tyndale.

McMinn, M. R., and B. W. McRay. 1997. "Spiritual Disciplines and the Practice of Integration: Possibilities and Challenges for Christian Psychologists." *Journal of Psychology and Theology* 251: 102–10.

Miller, J. K. 1987. *Sin: Overcoming the Ultimate Deadly Addiction*. San Francisco: Harper and Row.

Miller, W. R. 1999. *Integrating Spirituality into Treatment*. Washington, DC: American Psychological Association.

Miller, W. R. and C. E. Thoresen. 1999. "Spirituality and Health." In *Integrating Spirituality into Treatment*, edited by W. R. Miller, 3–18. Washington, DC: American Psychological Association.

Moberly, E. R. 1983. *Homosexuality: A New Christian Ethic*. Cambridge: James Clarke.

Monroe, P. G. 1997. "Building Bridges with Biblical Counselors." *Journal of Psychology and Theology* 251: 28–37.

Moore, W. L. 1983. *Courage and Confidence from the Bible: Inspiring Solutions to Your Deepest Problems*. Rev. ed. Chappaqua, NY: Christian Herald.

Morgan, C. T., R. A. King, and N. M. Robinson. 1979. *Introduction to Psychology*. 6th ed. New York: McGraw-Hill.

Narramore, S. B. 1997. "Psychology and Theology: Twenty-five Years of Theoretical Integration." *Journal of Psychology and Theology* 251: 6–10.

Niebuhr, H. R. 1951. *Christ and Culture*. New York: Harper and Row.

Oden, T. C. 1966. *Kerygma and Counseling*. Philadelphia: Westminster.

———. 1967. *Contemporary Theology and Psychotherapy*. Philadelphia: Westminster.

———. 1979. *Agenda for Theology*. New York: Harper and Row.

———. 1983. *Pastoral Theology: Essentials of Ministry*. San Francisco: Harper and Row.

———. 1984. *Care of Souls in the Classic Tradition*. Philadelphia, PA: Fortress.

———. 1987. *The Living God*. Vol. 1, *Systematic Theology*. New York: HarperSanFrancisco.

———. 1989. *Pastoral Counsel*. New York: Crossroad.

———. 1993. *The Transforming Power of Grace*. Nashville: Abingdon.

Ogletree, T. W. 1983. *The Use of the Bible in Christian Ethics*. Philadelphia: Fortress.

Packer, J. I., and T. Howard. 1985. *Christianity: The True Humanism*. Waco, TX: Word.

Pargament, K. I. 1997. *The Psychology of Religion and Coping: Theory, Research, Practice*. New York: Guilford.

Powlison, D. A. 1992. "Integration or Inundation?" In *Power Religion: The Selling Out of the Evangelical Church?* edited by M. S. Horton, 191–218. Chicago: Moody.

Richards, P. S., and A. E. Bergin. 2000. *Handbook of Psychotherapy and Religious Diversity.* Washington, DC: American Psychological Association.

Rinehart, S., and P. Rinehart. 1986. *How to Base Your Life on What Really Matters: Living in Light of Eternity.* Colorado Springs: NavPress.

Ross, G. 1994. *Treating Adolescent Substance Abuse: Understanding the Fundamental Elements.* Boston: Allyn and Bacon.

Schuller, R. H. 1982. *Self-Esteem: The New Reformation.* Waco, TX: Word.

Seamands, D. A. 1981. *Healing for Damaged Emotions.* Wheaton, IL: Victor.

Shafranske, E. P. 1996. *Religion and the Clinical Practice of Psychology.* Washington, DC: American Psychological Association.

———. 1996. "Religious Beliefs, Affiliations, and Practices of Clinical Psychologists." In *Religion and the Clinical Practice of Psychology,* edited by E. P. Shafranske, 149–62. Washington, DC: American Psychological Association.

Shelton, C. M. 1995. *Pastoral Counseling with Adolescents and Young Adults.* New York: Crossroad.

Shertzer, B., and S. C. Stone. 1968. *Fundamentals of Counseling.* Boston: Houghton Mifflin.

Smalley, G., and J. Trent. 1986. *The Blessing.* Nashville: Thomas Nelson.

———. 1987. *The Gift of Honor.* Nashville: Thomas Nelson.

———. 1988. *The Language of Love: A Powerful Way to Maximize Insight, Intimacy, and Understanding.* Pomona, CA: Focus on the Family.

Smith, D. L. 1992. *A Handbook of Contemporary Theology.* Wheaton, IL: Victor.

Swindoll, C. R. 1987. *The Quest for Character.* Portland: Multnomah.

"Theology." 2007. *The Columbia Electronic Encyclopedia.* New York: Columbia University Press. Available at http://www.infoplease.com/ce6/society/A0848415.html.

Thurneysen, E. 1962. *A Theology of Pastoral Care*. Translated by J. A. Worthington and T. Wieser. Richmond: John Knox.

Tisdale, T. S., S. E. Thealander, and P. L. Pike. 1997. "We Press toward the Goal." *Journal of Psychology and Theology* 251: 3–5.

Truax, C. B., and R. R. Carkhuff. 1967. *Toward Effective Counseling and Psychotherapy: Training and Practice*. Chicago: Aldine.

Van Deusen Hunsinger, D. 1995. *Theology and Pastoral Counseling: A New Interdisciplinary Approach*. Grand Rapids: Eerdmans.

Vande Kemp, H. 1996. "Historical Perspective: Religion and Clinical Psychology in America." In *Religion and the Clinical Practice of Psychology*, edited by E. P. Shafranske, 71–112. Washington, DC: American Psychological Association.

Wilson, W. P., and K. Slattery. 1984. *The Grace to Grow: The Power of Christian Faith in Emotional Healing*. Waco, TX: Word.

Wood, H. H. 1972. "Constructive Collaborators: Religion and Psychology." *Journal of Religion and Health* 112: 120–33.

Worthen, F. 1984. *Steps Out of Homosexuality*. San Rafael, CA: Love in Action.

Wulff, D. M. 1996. "The Psychology of Religion: An Overview." In *Religion and the Clinical Practice of Psychology*, edited by E. P. Shafranske, 43–70. Washington, DC: American Psychological Association.

Young-Eisendrath, P., and M. E. Miller, eds. 2000. *The Psychology of Mature Spirituality: Integrity, Wisdom, Transcendence*. London: Routledge.

www.ingramcontent.com/pod-product-compliance
Lightning Source LLC
Chambersburg PA
CBHW071437160426
43195CB00013B/1934